THE DISABLING STATE OF AN ACTIVE SOCIETY

Welfare and Society
Studies in Welfare Policy, Practice and Theory

Series Editors:
Matthew Colton, Kevin Haines, Peter Raynor and Susan Roberts
Swansea University, UK

Welfare and Society is an exciting series from the Department of Applied Social Science at Swansea University, in conjunction with Ashgate, concerned with all aspects of social welfare. The series publishes works of research, theory, history and practice from a wide range of contemporary applied social studies subjects such as Criminal Justice, Child Welfare, Community Care, Race and Ethnicity, Therapeutic and Intervention Techniques, Community Development and Social Policy. The series includes extended research reports of scholarly interest as well as works aimed at both the academic and professional communities.

The Disabling State of an Active Society

MIKAEL HOLMQVIST
Stockholm University, Sweden

ASHGATE

Published by
Ashgate Publishing Limited
Wey Court East
Union Road
Farnham
Surrey, GU9 7PT
England

Ashgate Publishing Company
Suite 420
101 Cherry Street
Burlington
VT 05401-4405
USA

www.ashgate.com

British Library Cataloguing in Publication Data
Holmqvist, Mikael, 1970-
   The disabling state of an active society. -- (Welfare and society
   1. Right to labor--Sweden. 2. Manpower policy--Sweden.
   3. Unemployed--Services for--Sweden--Case studies.
   4. Vocational rehabilitation--Sweden--Case studies.
   I. Title II. Series
   331.1'28'09485-dc22

Library of Congress Cataloging-in-Publication Data
Holmqvist, Mikael, 1970-
   The disabling state of an active society / by Mikael Holmqvist.
      p. cm. -- (Welfare and society)
   Includes bibliographical references and index.
   ISBN 978-0-7546-7832-8 (hardback) -- ISBN 978-0-7546-9645-2 (ebook) 1. People with disabilities--Employment--Sweden. 2. Employment subsidies--Sweden. 3. Welfare recipients--Employment--Sweden. 4. Social participation--Sweden. I. Title.

   HD7256.S9H65 2009
   362.4'048409485--dc22

2009015709

ISBN 9780754678328 (hbk)
ISBN 9780754696452 (ebk)

Mixed Sources
Product group from well-managed
forests and other controlled sources
www.fsc.org Cert no. SA-COC-1565
© 1996 Forest Stewardship Council

Printed and bound in Great Britain by
MPG Books Group, UK

Contents

For my son, Samuel Mikaelsson Lind

Preface

One of the most important ideological changes on the labor markets during recent years has been the discourse on 'employability.' This refers to individuals' ability to gain and maintain employment, and stresses their ability to be self-sufficient actors that draw on an appropriate set of skills, experiences and attitudes. The discourse concerns a transformation of responsibility for employment from society to the individual, and introduces the employable individual as a normative category with strong self-confidence and a will to act forcefully. In essence, the individual should act responsibly and independently, and take initiative. The discourse also concerns flexibility, as the individual is constantly required to adapt his or her behavior swiftly, effectively, and even happily, to the constantly changing requirements that characterize today's societies. Under such an approach, people's learning, adaptability and openness to change become critical. As Garsten and Jacobsson (2004: 1) put it:

> In today's competitive labor markets, employability and learning have been placed at the center of attention. In recruitment ads as well as in employment office documents; in corporate policies as well as in the policy recommendations of intergovernmental organizations, the significance of learning is underlined. Competence and skill are seen as perishable goods, of strategic value for individuals as well as organizations and even nations. Continuous learning is key to the successful navigation of individuals in labor markets. Learning is considered necessary in order to be employable. Even if working and learning are not new companions, this message speaks of a transition from a relatively stable pattern of work to more uncertain structural arrangements, with new demands placed on the individual. Many of these are posed by transnational organizations and with reference to market demands. A dominant idea is that getting a job, or being among the candidates for a job interview, is to a large degree dependent upon the power or initiative of the individual, upon one's own sense of responsibility for one's actions and decisions. The individual has to have certain characteristics: she must be "employable", "flexible" and be prepared to engage in "lifelong learning."

If we regard unemployment as the result of problems and deficiencies among people, government policies are likely to focus on changing individuals' attitudes and behaviors, rather than any structural issues. In such a world, people are to be 'rehabilitated,' 'reformed,' 'empowered,' 'cured' and 'normalized' through individual efforts of learning and change that are variations on the theme of 'activation.' But, as Bauman (2007) noted, by declaring them incapable of meeting the standards and norms of 'normal' conduct, the same society that seeks to enable 'disabled' people is also expert in branding them 'disabled.' In seeking to activate its citizens, societies may eventually disable them.

In completing this book, I have been offered much valuable advice from a number of colleagues: Konstantin Lampou, Richard Swedberg, Johan Hansson, Christian Maravelias, Per Skålén, Alexander Styhre, Peter Dobers, Dick Forslund and Hans Hasselbladh. I am also grateful to the two anonymous reviewers of the synopsis of this book. Some of the empirical findings that are reported here have previously been published in another book of mine (Holmqvist, 2008). Finally, I remain most obliged to my wife, Maria Lind.

Mikael Holmqvist
Stockholm, April 2009

Chapter 1

Introduction

In the early 1980s, stagnating Western economies were generally seen to push work organizations toward becoming more flexible and entrepreneurial by moving away from traditional hierarchical forms of governance to forms of governance that were built around individual subjects' self-governing capabilities and active participation. In that connection, traditional welfarism in the form of Keynesian economic interventions – aimed at securing full employment – and public benefit programs were increasingly criticized for breeding passivity and state dependency. In their place emerged forms of governance that stimulated rather than regulated the play of market forces, and that substituted (passive) public benefits for various active income supports.

Today, this interest has evolved into a complex multi-billion-euro network of organizations, programs and professional experts that are variations on the theme of "active society" (see, for example, Dean, 1995; Jensen and Pfau-Effinger, 2005; Walters, 1997). On average, the OECD countries allocate around 40 percent of their total labor market expenditures to active measures, but the empirical evidence about their efficacy is far from conclusive (see, for example, Calmfors et al., 2002; Fredriksson and Johansson, 2003; Janoski, 1990; Lange and Georgellis, 2007). Nevertheless, they are generally praised by many economists and politicians as useful tools in fighting unemployment: "There is widespread consensus among the OECD and EU countries about the blessings of the active society. The active society is perceived as the best or only way of combating poverty and social exclusion" (Elm Larsen, 2005: 135).

In the active society, jobseekers are expected to be "active" rather than "passive" recipients of financial aid. The activation model aims at "developing human capital and increasing the reserve workforce" as well as providing people "with moral skills, such as self-management, self-help and self-reliance, in order to create a new kind of worker who is more flexible, responsible and active" (Serrano Pascual, 2007: 23). According to Goul Andersen et al. (2005: vii), "active citizenship" implies the following:

> A new ideal of citizenship or a new set of rights and duties based on a conception of a claimant (e.g., an unemployed person) as an active citizen. The active citizen is granted more autonomy and choice but in return is assumed to be self-responsible, flexible and mobile.

Achieving activity is an individual responsibility, but it is also a matter of concern for society, for example through various welfare-to-work programs (Lindert, 2004;

Saunders, 2005). The phrase 'empowerment of the unemployed' designates this enterprise. It is concerned with enabling unemployed citizens to eventually control their own lives, hence achieving a kind of 'reformation to normal life' (see, for example, Abberley, 2002; Albrecht et al., 2001; De Lathouwer, 2005). Gilbert (2005: 15) says: "Activation policies are largely geared to changing workers" – they are focused on transforming humans' potential for employability (Garsten and Jacobsson, 2004). In general, activation aims to turn the presumed passive and more or less excluded unemployed person into an energetic, able and included citizen (see Kvist, 2002; Van Berkel et al., 2002). Government-sponsored activities for the integration of the unemployed in working life are favored by a number of prominent international organizations, such as the United Nations International Labor Organization (UNLO), the World Health Organization (WHO), the Organization for Economic Cooperation and Development (OECD) and the European Union (EU), as well as by several non-government organizations, such as Workability International. Likewise, single governments, lobby organizations and commercial industries in many countries favor activating labor market policies (see Abrahamson and Oorschot, 2003; Glennerster, 1999; Kvist, 2002; Lødemel and Trickey, 2000; Hvinden et al., 2001; Oorschot and Hvinden, 2001; Overbye, 2005).

An active society is one that ensures people can work, and enables them to do so: "'Active measures' comprise practical efforts to assist people to find or remain in paid employment and thus improve their prospects in the labor market" (Hvinden et al., 2001: 169). The concept is based on the idea that "employment is the 'royal road' to combating exclusion and promoting inclusion" (Van Berkel et al., 2002: 33). By strengthening people's skills, competencies and overall employability, jobseekers become ready and able to work when opportunities are available, hence avoiding the pitfalls of creating a permanent underclass of recipients of welfare aid (see Garraty, 1978; Walters, 1997). As Dean (1995: 579) concluded: "Contemporary social policy has devised a range of institutional conditions and governmental means by which the active subject could be formed" in order to fight the specter of the self-reproduction of "a dependent group permanently living within the welfare system." During recent years in many welfare countries, there has been "a shift from *passive* to *active* measures, an emphasis on individuals' *responsibilities* to be self-sufficient vis-à-vis citizens' *rights* to social benefits, and a redefinition of policy objectives from *income maintenance* to *social inclusion*" (Gilbert, 2005: 9). Elm Larsen (2005: 137) observes:

> Most European welfare states have adopted some kind of activation policy in their overall unemployment policy. The new active line in labor market and social policy has been introduced under different names in the different European welfare states. These active measures have been of prime importance in reforming welfare systems and in stimulating or forcing labor-market participation of the unemployed and other social benefits claimants.

One example of this is the New Labour program in the United Kingdom during the late 1990s:

> The Blair [Tony Blair, former Prime Minister] project is to modernize the welfare state; to turn it into an 'active' welfare state that promotes personal responsibility and individual opportunity as opposed to what is characterized as a 'passive' welfare state that encourages dependency and lack of initiative. Blair has made clear that reform is not just about reining in expenditure, but about a fundamental change in the 'culture, attitude and practice of the welfare state.' (Lister, 1998: 224).

Overall, an 'active line' toward the unemployed stresses how governments want to instill a new kind of responsibility where needy people activate themselves in order to become 'normal citizens' – people fulfilling certain obligations as part of a societal contract (Van Berkel and Hornemann Moller, 2002). This is thought to be the primary means through which unemployed people become employable. As Dean (1995: 572) argues:

> An 'active system' of income support for the unemployed not only acts upon the financial plight of the unemployed, and upon their job prospects, but also upon those attitudes, affects, conduct and dispositions that present a barrier to the unemployed returning to the labor market, and alienate them from social networks and obligations.

As Van Berkel and Hornemann Moller (2002: 62) note, activation programs for combating unemployment have a distinctly positive aura. The focus is on helping people to help themselves through rehabilitation, empowerment, training and so on. Obviously, as they state, such a program must become a popular one:

> One of the most striking phenomena of the introduction of the active approach is the widespread rhetorical support for it. Activation policies are among those rare policy issues that receive support from almost the entire political spectrum.

Despite much recent attention from scholars and politicians to the merits of 'the active welfare state,' so far few if any systematic studies have been proposed into the effects the interest in activation programs have had on the unemployed people who come into contact with them, or on the general social and welfare problems of unemployment in an active society (cf. Abrahamson and Oorschot, 2003; Hansen et al., 2002). There are many valuable labor market statistics available on the extent of unemployment and the kind of activity offered; often these data are provided in detail, categorized by age, ethnicity, sex, occupation, local conditions and other factors. There is also an interesting anecdotal literature on social issues; unemployed people have effectively described their careers in the active society.

But there is generally a gap between the bare figures of statistics and the literary accounts, open as they might be to all kinds of fortuitous interpretations.

The purpose of this book is to bridge this gap by studying a particular activation program – Samhall – in a particular country, Sweden. Samhall is an organization that employs "occupationally disabled people" and offers them work in order to improve their employability. The activation programs are particularly focused on supporting disadvantaged groups, such as people with disabilities (see Abberley, 2002; Drake, 1999; OECD, 2003; Oorschot and Hvinden, 2001; Overbye, 2005). These programs are thought to increase their chances of leaving a life of social exclusion, reducing their stigmatized status as secondary social citizens as well as increasing their health and well-being (see Corker and Shakespeare, 2002; Oorschot and Hvinden, 2001; Shildrick and Price, 1996; Wadensjö, 2007). The active society invites disabled people into full participation, asking for their skills, competencies and capabilities. As students of disability policies have noted, this is a fundamentally new societal approach to this group of people (see Albrecht et al., 2001; Drake, 1999).

Internationally, Sweden is often considered a model welfare state pursuing an activation policy that has been the subject of much interest (see, for example, Lindert, 2004; Saunders, 2005; Van Berkel and Hornemann Moller, 2002); Samhall can be seen as the crown jewel in that system. Swedish (and Scandinavian) employment rates have for many years been among the highest in the world, implying a successful approach to activating jobseekers, for example by offering them employment with Samhall. As Van Berkel and Hornemann Moller (2002: 51) describe it:

> Countries differ with respect to their tradition of developing measures to promote participation. The Nordic countries are among those countries with a relatively long tradition in this respect. Active labor-market policies in Sweden, particularly, have been closely related to the commitment to maintain a high level of employment, preferably full employment.

Of course, Samhall is deeply embedded in a unique political, social and economic context – Swedish welfare. This issue can fruitfully be explored in considerable detail given the important research that exists on Swedish welfare and its unique characteristics, for example by placing Samhall in a historical context, thus acknowledging its links to active labor market policy since the period between the two world wars, or by comparing Samhall's activities to other Swedish social welfare programs.

In this book, however, I choose to address this system's relevance to the international debate about the welfare state by examining the activation logic upon which the practices of Samhall and other countries' welfare programs currently rely. The topic is interesting and relevant to developments in the career chances of those jobseekers who come to be socially organized as 'people with disabilities' in Europe and elsewhere. Samhall draws on an activating discourse, respecting the 'active line' in European welfare policy in order to empower and rehabilitate disabled people into able citizens. This book not only tries to address the design and consequences of a particular activation program in a particular country, it also aims to contribute to a general understanding of the effects the interest in activation programs has on the disabled people that come into contact with them.

Methods

In December 2002, I contacted Samhall's CEO and proposed to undertake a study of how Samhall's occupationally disabled employees were recruited and put to work. As a student of organization with a particular interest in individual change and learning, I was intrigued by Samhall's mission to activate individuals with occupational disability. Thus, I explained to him that I was a scholar with a particular interest in learning more about how people with occupational disabilities develop in Samhall. He agreed to the project, and assigned four of his deputies to act as my contact group. Most of the research was carried out during 2003–2005, with some complementary activities during 2006–2007. Throughout the project I acted as an independent researcher, and at no time did Samhall interfere with my activities, at least as far as I am aware. The contact group initiated some contacts in the organization to help me get started. Soon, however, they allowed me to make any contacts I felt important without having to check with anyone. My informants often helped me to contact other important informants, both within and outside Samhall. The study was funded by a research grant from two national research foundations in Sweden without any obligations to Samhall. Overall, Samhall had no influence on the design of my study.

Open-ended interviews, semi-overt participant observation and archival data were the three main data collection techniques used in the present research, where I have tried to observe events, listen to statements, ask questions in informal conversations and in formal interviews, participate in activities and ceremonies, and read relevant written materials.

Interviews

I conducted 119 open-ended interviews (Silverman, 2006): 25 with administrative officials of the National Employment Office [1](NEO – the agency responsible for assigning unemployed people to employment with Samhall), 5 with members of Samhall's top management team, 30 with supervisors and local branch managers, and 59 with occupationally disabled employees. Interviews were theoretically sampled (Strauss and Corbin, 1998) to represent various social, medical and organizational categories – men and women, physically and mentally impaired, senior members and newcomers, staff and employees, and so on. Following Lincoln

---

1 In the original Swedish, 'Arbetsförmedlingen'.

and Guba's (1985) guidelines for "purposeful sampling" in choosing informants, my overall aim was to find people who would be best able to inform me about my research question. Of particular interest were the occupationally disabled people's experiences of the organization and its practices: for instance, how did they regard themselves in terms of health and illness; how did they perceive their rehabilitation and development; how did they experience their efforts to exit Samhall?

These interviews focused on understanding the categories used by Samhall (for example, disability and rehabilitation) from the standpoint of the employees. Most of the interviews with the occupationally disabled employees were carried out during practical work or during breaks, and could hence involve the presence of colleagues and supervisors. On average, interviews lasted around 40–60 minutes. My questions focused on the career stages that employees of Samhall undergo, and I tried to understand how the different stages would affect employees' self-image as occupationally disabled. When interviewing supervisors, I asked them how they introduced newcomers, and I asked employees how they experienced this introduction. I also spent a lot of time trying to understand how both supervisors and employees thought about the character of the work offered by Samhall and how this work could affect organization members' self-image. Further, I asked questions regarding job rotation, counseling and other activities related to the idea that "Samhall activates its employees through a developing and meaningful work environment," as is suggested in one of the organization's brochures. Overall, questions were broad, but once themes began to emerge across interviews, for example regarding the character of work, they were validated in subsequent interviews (Spradley, 1979). As an example of this, during my pilot study of about seven weeks, my questions were much more general and tentative than during the main study, when my "sensitivity" to the case had increased (Strauss and Corbin, 1998).

Participant Observation

In addition, semi-overt participant observation was conducted (Hammersley and Atkinson, 1995; Spradley 1979). I conducted observation at ten sites located in different regions in Sweden, four of which were visited during two periods (see the Appendix). The sites were suggested to me by my contacts at Samhall. They respected my request that the sites reflect operations both in cities and in the countryside, as well as the production of both goods and services. I did not find that the sites were chosen to represent any particular aspect of Samhall's activities; overall, they gave me a general picture of the organization. To gain some verification regarding this, I consulted a number of Samhall magazines distributed to the employees that reported on the situation in Samhall, at least as it was portrayed by Samhall itself. I also studied some government reports on Samhall, which provided additional information on the company and its clients.

Each observation period lasted about ten working days. Upon entrance at each site, I was introduced by the plant manager as a researcher from a university. Some managers stressed that I had "understood what Samhall was all about," and that the clients should feel relaxed in their interaction with me. During my study, information was posted on Samhall's internal Website about my research project, thus indicating that it was undertaken "with the blessing of top management." This piece of information seemed to be more necessary in relation to supervisors and plant managers than to the clients. Perhaps even some clients initially looked upon me with some suspicion, as some of them, as it appeared to me, remained hostile to Samhall as an organization. Overall, however, I was well accommodated by the clients in the different work groups, particularly after having described my project in less formal terms and on a more personal basis.

During my time at each site, I wore the same clothes as the occupationally disabled employees, ate lunch with them, took coffee breaks with them and so on. On three occasions I was invited to live in employees' homes during my whole stay. Essentially, my goal was to work as an ordinary employee. Depending on the type of work at the site, I participated in a host of activities, such as cleaning, maintenance, archival work, production of food and manufacture of furniture (see the Appendix for more details). During work, I chatted with employees about Samhall, about their careers, and in particular about their jobs. The approach was necessarily tentative, even though more specific questions were asked as themes emerged (Spradley, 1979). Observational activities were important to gain some deeper understanding of what was going on in Samhall, how people looked upon themselves, how their careers progressed, how the supervisors organized the work, and so on. The statements by employees and supervisors and my personal impressions were written down in a notebook as verbatim and as close to the event as possible. The notebook was transcribed once a week. Overall, my participant observation became all the more structured and focused as themes emerged, for example regarding how meetings were held with employees, or how work was organized and carried out.

Archival Data

Three sources of archival data were gathered.[2] The first source of information was the Samhall staff magazine, *Samhall i Fokus* ("Samhall in Focus"). The second source of information was ten government reports on Samhall that had been published between 1980 and 2005, *Statens Offentliga Utredningar* (SOU – "The State's Official Enquiries"). By and large, these reports of about 200 pages each consisted of studies of Samhall's economic dealings, its ability to reach its official goals, and comments upon the organization of work. The third source of

---

2   For the sake of simplicity, and since all the written sources (government reports on Samhall, internal Samhall documents and so on) are only available in the original Swedish, in the following I only refer to them by stating what type of source is being used in the particular case – for example, "According to a government report, Samhall ..."; "One Samhall document emphasized the following ...." For readers with a command of Swedish, a complete list of written sources is available in Holmqvist (2005: 403–34).

information was books about Samhall written by Samhall employees (see Aulin, 2001) or ex-employees. For instance, one former press relations officer published a book in 1990 where she gave a personal account of her experiences of working as a manager for Samhall (see Rådahl, 1990). All written materials were in Swedish.

Outline

The book is organized as follows.

In Chapter 2, I introduce the Samhall labor market program and describe its aim of activating jobseekers who are regarded as "occupationally disabled." Disabled people are commonly seen as the most difficult group to employ in Sweden and internationally; hence, they are the subject of the most intensive empowerment initiatives in order to help them become self-sufficient and 'able' again. The chapter is largely devoted to the rhetoric of Samhall, presenting ideas on empowerment and rehabilitation of disabled people through work.

In Chapter 3, I describe how jobseekers are identified as "occupationally disabled" by the National Employment Office in order to become eligible for help from the Swedish welfare state. Once coded as disabled, a jobseeker can be assigned activation by Samhall. The chapter focuses on how an activating welfare state identifies who should be empowered, and how this can be accomplished.

In Chapter 4, I report on the entry procedures to Samhall – quite simply, what kind of an 'organizational world' the jobseekers initially confront when being assigned to this program that aims to empower and integrate them into society. The individual is confronted with a particular organization that emphasizes his or her disabilities and how they are to be resolved through participation in various training programs and practical work. The chapter describes how a welfare organization tries to realize the active society by offering a particular work environment designed to rehabilitate and empower a needy and excluded person.

Chapter 5 describes how the newly employed client is organized initially by Samhall. Samhall devotes much attention to establishing what kind of mental or physical problems the individual is suffering from in order to prepare for an "individually adapted" activation. The client is encouraged to reveal his or her problems in what is deemed a significant exercise in order to provide the best possible help. Based on the extent of the problems identified by Samhall (grounded in information given by the NEO that has previously classified the client as disabled), the organization prepares the client for his or her new career as occupationally disabled. The ultimate goal is to develop a successful career with Samhall that leads to the client exiting the organization as non-disabled.

In Chapter 6, I describe how Samhall places the client in an appropriate position in any of its many facilities or external assignments (such as cleaning, maintenance, information technology work or manufacture of industrial products) based on the problems he or she is alleged to suffer from and that are to be resolved through the work offered. The organization argues that in order for the disabled individual to become rehabilitated and empowered, he or she must be given appropriate tasks based on the limitations that have been identified. The chapter describes how people are placed in different work groups depending on their 'disability' – insufficient language skills, sight impairment, alleged intellectual impairments, and so on.

In Chapter 7, I relate how Samhall's activation program is based on the idea that occupationally disabled people develop best in work teams rather than working alone. Thus all occupationally disabled employees are placed in work groups that carry out different assignments, such as production of food, cleaning, maintenance and factory work. In theory, there should be job rotation within and between the teams in order to activate the client and prepare him or her for a job outside Samhall. In reality, however, teams remain permanent, as do work tasks. Clients are rewarded for working repetitively. Samhall's supervisors argue that developing in permanent teams is the best means to accomplish successful rehabilitation, as they assume that disabled people in general do not want changes in work content.

Chapter 8 expands on this by focusing on the content of the work. Following a theory of adapting work content to the presumed needs of disabled people, clients are offered very simple and repetitive work. They are expected to grow and develop through strict work routines. These routines are said to be 'activating' by teaching the client a repetitive mode of behavior. I offer accounts of how the work content affects the clients – most of them believe that the longer they stay at Samhall, the more disabled they become, through a kind of lock-in effect.

In Chapter 9, I report how, as the career of an occupationally disabled employee at Samhall progresses, the employees experience that they become all the more 'competent' as disabled in their professional roles. They become more attuned to the activation program offered by Samhall – not least as a result of the division of labor, where different groups of disabled people learn from experience certain competencies and skills that are relevant to their roles as disabled. Through positive feedback between experience and competence, jobseekers eventually learn how to act as occupationally disabled as a result of the work they are engaged in.

Chapter 10 turns to the question of the interplay between the occupationally disabled employee who is to be rehabilitated and the Samhall supervisor responsible for this enterprise. A number of issues are discussed, such as supervisors' attitudes toward the disabled that affect how they are approached, what kinds of activities the supervisors believe are appropriate for them, and how supervisors perceive their role as leaders for a group of people that have been labeled 'incapacitated.' Supervisors are required to implement Samhall's rehabilitation policy, and are therefore vital actors. The general emphasis among the supervisors is to "motivate the supervisor" – helping disabled employees to realize that they have problems, and helping them to resolve them.

Chapter 11 devotes attention to how Samhall tries to shelter its occupationally disabled employees from much of 'real life's' complexity. This takes the form of offering the employees a slower working tempo and very simple assignments, emphasizing working 'with your hands' rather than 'with your head,' and so on. These practices are based on Samhall's intention to help employees to develop given their presumed problems in terms of limited mental and physical capacities. This ideology is based on good intentions, according to which the employee is to eventually develop into a more secure, strong and able character. However, an unanticipated consequence is that the employees become even more unable to function successfully outside Samhall.

Chapter 12 focuses on how occupationally disabled employees accommodated by Samhall are encouraged to learn about each other personally by talking about the reasons why they are there, for example in group discussions focusing on each employee's assumed problems and limitations or in regular conversations with supervisors. A 'disability culture' that is pervasive among the older employees affects new employees as soon as they enter Samhall. Older employees acting as 'competent models' invite new employees into a kind of 'disabled fellowship.' Moreover, Samhall regularly conveys to its disabled employees that they are unique due to their impairments, and that Samhall is a unique organization designed to help them. In general, this chapter reports how Samhall clients' careers progress in a somewhat 'disabled' fashion by learning the ropes of an organization that focuses on their problems and limitations.

Chapter 13 looks at how Samhall judges employees to be 'non-disabled,' and thus eligible for a new life outside Samhall, and how employees try to leave the organization. It describes how employees are encouraged to find a job outside Samhall, and how supervisors at Samhall, together with officers at the NEO, try to achieve this aim. Samhall's goal is to have a yearly turnover of occupationally disabled employees of 5 percent, but in reality only around 2–3 percent of employees leave, most of whom enter other welfare programs, such as wage allowance schemes, thus remaining on welfare support until they retire.

Chapter 14 discusses the reasons why most of Samhall's clients do not leave the activation program it offers. A central observation is that they have become convinced that they are suffering from the mental and/or physical problems that were said to be the reasons for their assignment to Samhall. Occupationally disabled employees testify that they cannot leave Samhall, and do not want to do so, and supervisors find it very hard to convince them to act differently. Paradoxically, by having been activated as a welfare-disabled client, they appear to have become incapacitated and passive.

Chapter 15 reports on the mismatch between Samhall's intentions and the experiences of the occupationally disabled employees. Despite the goal of providing a meaningful and stimulating work environment, the contrary is typically the case, and may contribute to explaining why few people who enter Samhall become more employable.

Finally, Chapter 16 offers conclusions from the study, and proposes the implications for research into the active society.

Chapter 2
Samhall: A Popular Activation Program

A Samhall video sets out the organization's philosophy: "Every society has to acknowledge some fundamental rights – one is the right to employment. Everyone can contribute to the common well-being. This is the basis for our co-existence, the momentum behind our well-being, or society will fall apart." Expanding on this idea, one of Samhall's brochures emphasizes that "Samhall's activities are based on the fundamental value that all people have equal value and the same right to work." Echoing much international debate on the empowerment of disabled people through work, according to Samhall work is: "of major significance for the quality of our lives and for our participation in society. It is not just about work as a source of our livelihood, but much more a means to fellowship, meaning and development in our existence." The idea that welfare recipients become autonomous, self-responsible and eventually employable through various welfare programs is central to the Swedish welfare state's active line regarding unemployment benefits.

Today, Samhall is one of Scandinavia's largest corporations. It employs around 22,000 individuals and has a turnover of approximately 900 million euros. Fully owned by the Swedish state, it is Sweden's leading subcontractor, selling goods and services to companies, government agencies and municipalities. Well-known international partners include IKEA, Ericsson, ABB and AstraZeneca, to mention but a few. Samhall also sells a range of its own products, both on the Swedish and international markets. As an important feature of contemporary Swedish labor market policy, it is an organization that recruits those who are least attractive to employers – occupationally disabled people. An occupationally disabled person is an individual who has difficulties getting or keeping a job, due to functional disorders that present a handicap in relation to other people on the labor market. Therefore, he or she is assigned employment at Samhall by the Swedish state.

Besides offering occupationally disabled people employment under the same conditions as in any other Swedish company, Samhall's purpose is to provide "professional and personal rehabilitation, for instance, strengthening of self-confidence, increasing independence and developing valuable competence," as stated in one of Samhall's brochures. Hence, Samhall constitutes an example of an activation program that aims "to transform disability into ability," as suggested by the OECD (see OECD, 2003). One Samhall document emphasizes that "Samhall is an opportunity for personal and professional development through work for people with occupational disabilities." As mentioned above, the ultimate goal is that the period of employment at Samhall should end: "Work within Samhall is organized in such a way that it enables the employee to eventually find employment with another employer." Hence, a government study observed that Samhall has a special role "in society's rehabilitation activities," and pointed out that "the rehabilitation undertaking must be regarded as being central to Samhall's activities." This is said to imply "helping sick people and people with a functional disorder to obtain the best functional capacity possible and conditions for a normal life ... aimed at people who for medical, social or other reasons have difficulties in obtaining and retaining a job."

An issue that has been debated over the years is an alleged increase in the commercialization of Samhall, which some assume will impose tougher demands on employees and push Samhall further away from providing the sheltered environment that has traditionally been its goal. In the debate, it has been maintained, "There is a conflict between the commercial assignment and the responsibility for those who have the greatest difficulty on the labor market," and that "the criticism against Samhall is that there is too much focus on the economy," as a government investigator put it. Presumably, this has generally led to a more stressful work situation for the disabled employees. A member of the Swedish Parliament wrote about Samhall:

> At one time, Samhall was founded to take care of society's weakest. This operational concept must never be set aside. Naturally, it is only logical that Samhall should earn some money, but not at any price. Today, the demand for profitability is pushing the enterprise to becoming a company competing with private industry.

A recent radio report maintained that during recent years, Samhall has been severely criticized and "the company has been accused of pushing the occupationally disabled too hard," purely from motives of maximizing profitability. In another radio program, the latest government investigator of Samhall said:

> The Government's control of Samhall has resulted in contradictory impulses. On the one hand, Samhall has requirements for profitability, efficiency like other companies. On the other hand Samhall must ensure that it takes good care of its employees, activating them and making sure that they get new jobs. These things just don't seem compatible.

He further developed his line of argument in an interview in Samhall's staff magazine: "There is a conflict between the demands for profitability that exist today at Samhall and the mandate to activate people with functional disorders." Consequently, similar arguments were presented in the study the investigator was in charge of: "In conformity with earlier studies, this study establishes that there is an obvious conflict in goals between the demands for profitability and the requirements for offering persons with occupational disabilities meaningful and stimulating work," and that "business activities are a *prerequisite* for [Samhall's] labor market policy and social assignments. At the same time, this is where *the conflict* in the assignment lies."

Via so-called state compensation for additional costs, the Swedish Parliament provides Samhall with a certain amount of funding each year, which is budgeted in terms of hours. Compensation for additional costs amounts to a little more than 500,000 euros that Samhall receives from the government in order to be able to offer activities adapted to the occupationally disabled. According to the most recent government study on Samhall, the system is based on the fact that Samhall receives a fixed amount of compensation regardless of which kinds of people are recruited. Those with grave established disabilities do not receive more compensation than those with less serious ones. Samhall's first CEO (who held the post for twenty years) explained that compensation for additional costs is based on the fact that "the state will compensate the company for the additional costs; it is not a per capita calculation." The most recent government report on Samhall sets out the structure of the system for compensation for additional costs. In this study, it emerges that, among other things, compensation for additional costs doubled while the total revenues for the same years trebled. The percentage of compensation for additional costs of the total revenues has thus gone down over the entire period.

For instance, the Annual Report for 2006 reported, "for the financial years 2003 and 2004, a volume of at least 27.3 and 26.4 million work hours respectively have been stipulated for employees with occupational disabilities," and all jobs are calculated in hours at the different work places. One work place with approximately 80 employees could thus budget approximately 70,000 "occupationally disabled hours" per year (the latest government study on Samhall reported that the state contributed 513,000 euros in compensation for additional costs corresponding to an employment requirement of 28.5 million work hours, and that the normal annual work time for a full-time job at Samhall is approximately 1,800 hours). A supervisor explained: "We make note of the time for each job. We keep a check on the hours and what we do with the hours." An occupationally disabled employee stressed: "On the regular labor market they count in euros, but we count hours here. What kind of signals does this send?" He was of the opinion that this creates a feeling within Samhall that as long as people are kept busy, or as long as they are present at the work place for certain a number of hours, the goal of producing "a number of thousands of occupationally disabled hours per unit" is achieved. To that extent, the work time itself, the organized employment, may take a prominent place in the company, but not the content of the work.

In essence, the compensation for extra costs paid out by the state to Samhall is based on the idea that "Samhall cannot freely select manpower, but has people with occupational disabilities assigned by the National Employment Office (NEO). In this connection, the lower productivity of the target group (working pace, working hours, absence and so on) as well as support resources (line and staff personnel, Corporate Health Service, work environment/work adaptation ...)" is the formal expression for the sheltered activities Samhall should carry out. During a meeting with his personnel, one supervisor emphasized: "You know that Samhall receives compensation for additional costs for your rehabilitation and your development," and continued: "There is a reason for this, namely that you are sick and disabled." A former CEO of Samhall said that the basis for compensation for additional costs when this system was instituted:

> was that the functionally disabled who obtained employment at Samhall should produce goods and services like other companies and at other work places. This would entail it becoming an enterprise that operated at a loss, as these were people who could not compete with other people on the open labor market. The compensation for additional costs would compensate for the lower production pace; that activation was built into the work place.

A supervisor for the Samhall employees working on a staffing assignment (where Samhall's occupationally disabled staff were hired out to other employers) explained that Samhall's approach to managing both business and personal development requirements for the occupationally disabled was to concentrate on simple assignments: "We take the simpler assignments so that they [companies which Samhall serves] can take the more difficult ones." A member of Samhall's corporate management felt that more and more people in Sweden "are becoming educated, that's quite true, but there are an awful lot of assignments in this country that have to be carried out in the country and which are of a simple nature, but there are not many people wanting to do them." Here he saw an important future market for Samhall: "In California, there are many illegal immigrants from Mexico who take the sorts of jobs we can offer … labor-intensive jobs." One supervisor explained: "Samhall can compete on the market for unskilled personnel."

The fact that a government study concluded that occupationally disabled people have more monotonous and simple jobs than other employees is hardly surprising: that is what people think is appropriate for them. A CD-ROM distributed by Samhall points out that the labor market "is often more stressful for people with functional disorders than for others. People with functional disorders often report that they work with monotonous assignments, in noisy environments, and think that work is stressful and monotonous. They also have less influence over their work." Further, it ascertained that outside Samhall, "employees with occupational disabilities get poorer jobs, they are often underemployed, are not allowed to do themselves justice, have limited social contracts," and that "others make decisions for employees with occupational disabilities. They themselves are accustomed to not complaining about unsatisfactory conditions."

However, it has become increasingly difficult for Samhall to be able to offer more 'simple types' of jobs for which the occupationally disabled are considered suitable, since many of these jobs are subject to competition from low-price countries. A Swedish Radio report titled "What will happen to the B team?" focused on "the occupationally disabled and functionally disordered always making up the B team on the labor market," who, when they have work, perform the simplest and most basic chores within industry. The report took up the problem of the increase in competition from low-price countries for the traditional simple jobs offered by Samhall: "Many of the simpler industrial jobs that previously made up the backbone of Samhall's activities are today placed out in the Baltic countries or in the Far East." The reporter went on to declare:

> This summer, a government study has proposed that the state should attract other companies than the state-owned Samhall to offer so-called sheltered work for those not thought to have a place in the A team. At the same time, thousands of the simple assembly and packaging jobs that these groups work on are disappearing each year to the Baltic countries and the Far East.

An administrative official at the NEO declared that there are many "such disabilities where people function at their best carrying out these kinds of jobs. If the simple packaging jobs no longer exist and are no longer available at Samhall, there is a large group of people that will not be able to get onto the labor market." Another administrative official there related that Samhall has always been popular among colleagues since it has even able to offer employment to people who have not been considered capable of carrying out advanced jobs: "The jobs out on the market have become more and more complex, and consequently more and more people are not qualified for them," he declared. In his opinion, "many of them I would assess as being presumptive Samhall cases, they are exactly the people we have here." In this connection, a supervisor at a Samhall work place regretted the transformation of society toward more knowledge-intensive industries: "In earlier times, our employees worked with somewhat simpler assignments in normal industries. They worked at the factories, cleaning, pottering around and so on."

With time, the labor-intensive jobs traditionally offered at Samhall's various industrial workshops have moved over to a growing service industry, where Samhall offers domestic services such as food purchasing for retired citizens, cleaning in homes and gardening, as well as jobs commissioned by other organizations by hiring out its personnel to other companies. For example, this can involve managing a factory storeroom, building maintenance and street cleaning, or working within the home-help service. However, Samhall's growing concentration on service and staffing jobs has been criticized as being too complex for the occupationally disabled. An NEO administrative official pointed out: "Samhall's employees need security, need to have simple routines, and staffing assignments aren't suitable for this," or as the Swedish National Audit Office expressed it in a study about Samhall: "Social competence is in short supply among the ... jobseekers that make up Samhall's target group. According to our assessment, there is consequently a risk that the current direction of service production, where social competence is necessary, may push aside Samhall's target group." A supervisor working on assignments where Samhall's personnel worked externally, for example as cleaners, believed: "Staffing is good for some of them, but not for the large masses [of employees], as social competence is required when working with healthy people." Since "normal work places" are not the sheltered environments that Samhall can offer, "the work can become far to complex and difficult for the majority of employees," another supervisor pointed out. However, a member of Samhall's corporate management thought: "It's better when people can get out and work in open environments and meet people in society." This was also maintained in Samhall's staff magazine: "Trying out a job outside Samhall while still retaining one's security and employment in Samhall provides many with increased self-confidence."

A Promise of a Better Life

An information video about Samhall begins with a journey through the Milky Way, where an embryo in a woman's womb looms large, accompanied by the commentary:

> Faith is not always fair. A newborn child holds the promise of the future. However, for some of us, the future seems less promising. I may be born with a serious disability, making my life very special indeed. Alternatively, perhaps, faith strikes me through accidents, changing all and every plan I've made. On the other hand, my mind may have a way of its own, plunging me into the deepest shadows of my soul. Yet I belong here. I have a contribution to make.

During the vignette, "Samhall: The Company of Opportunities," the narrator states: "I know faith has chosen a special life for me. I have sometimes despaired and there's no turning back. However, I can see another future now. I can see options and possibilities. I am proud. I am alive."

A former CEO of Samhall explained:

> During the twenty years I have been active in Samhall, we wanted to see Samhall as an opportunity for the disabled to gain access to the labor market, in part because we thought that the work in itself was enriching because it is worthwhile to belong to a social organization, in part to have an activity. Even if you can't always manage as much as other people, it is important to be a part of working life …. The alternative for these people is not only long-term sickness, but perhaps even long-term disability pension, and so we felt that it was more advantageous for society that people were at work than passively receiving disability pensions.

This idea is also stressed in one of Samhall's documents:

> A functional disorder can result in the individual being shut out or having difficulties in taking part in social fellowship. A job can then be of great value for the individual. We know that a person who is placed outside working life risks becoming passive and isolated. In turn, this leads to an increased need for

disability pensions, medical care, social welfare and so on, and thus increased costs for society.

The CEO of Samhall observed: "The major problem with our employees is self-confidence – self-confidence has taken a few blows. Our employees have been the subjects of analyses and surveys, practical occupational experience and other actions, perhaps experiencing repeated failure again. Perhaps self-confidence is the thing that separates success from non-success in life." The Samhall staff magazine and other Samhall publications report that many of the occupationally disabled employees at Samhall lacked self-confidence when they started work there. Reportedly, this stems from personal failure during previous employment, abuse, social maladjustment, loneliness, illness and so on. One man stated in a report in the staff magazine: "Earlier, I probably had very little self-confidence." However, he believed that the work he carried out at Samhall was good for his self-confidence and his self-image. A similar view was emphasized in another report: "'I think that my self-confidence is better since starting at Samhall. I now go [to work] with my fiancée. I met her at Samhall,' says Benny proudly turning the ring shining on his left ring finger."

Some of the occupationally disabled employees recount the hardships of having been unemployed for long periods, where feelings of worthlessness, isolation and resignation were common. In a report in the staff magazine, one of the employees explained: "Being at home was sending me crazy." Another report described the positive feeling of having obtained work at Samhall: "Before Benny came to Samhall, he was out of work for a year. It was terrible, he says. Days became nights and nights became days. The whole of my existence was in turmoil. I need routine and want a job where I can feel I am of use." One of the occupationally disabled employees said: "Samhall gives me the energy to carry on fighting, to become a part of society. There's no sense in just sitting at home." In the same article, a colleague of his explained: "When I work, I forget about my illness. When I'm at home I just sit thinking about it, then I become mentally tired." In a radio report, another occupationally disabled employee said:

> It's hard to find work, and it is harder for those that are ill than those that are healthy. However, I don't want to complain about anyone or anything. I'm happy to have a job. It's great that I can manage on my own. Perhaps this will strike someone as funny since I am a civil engineer, but I am very proud to be working as a cleaner. I'm happy, my boss is happy and the customer is happy.

Various Samhall publications carry similar accounts from a number of occupationally disabled employees describing how thankful they are for their employment at Samhall. For example, an advertising supplement in a Swedish newspaper featured a woman who said: "Without Samhall I would have become the recipient of a disability pension." Now she was a part-time driver for a county governor, which she referred to as a "dream job." The introduction to the article states that she suffered from "repetitive strain injuries to the neck and shoulders," which is why she started work at Samhall thirteen years earlier, when nobody wanted to offer employment to "someone who was so racked with pain." The employee pointed out that she still had pain "and takes painkillers every day," but thanks to Samhall "giving me self-confidence," she now had an agreeable working life: "I love driving and wanted to become a professional driver when I was young, but didn't really believe that I would be able to manage it." In an article in one of the annual reports dealing with a woman working in one of Samhall's packing industries, the woman relates:

> my supervisor is there if I need help with different things. For example, he supports me attending an AA group so that I can handle my relationship with alcohol. Overall, I feel very safe and secure at Samhall. I have grown familiar with the job and the climate here. It feels great with the support of my workmates. Here I work to the best of my ability, which can vary from time to time. It just wouldn't work for me at any other work place.

The fact that employees are, broadly speaking, pleased with their work tasks and employment is testified to by several of them in Samhall publications. An article in the latest annual report carries a story about one woman:

> She feels safe and secure with her work tasks and gets on well. – "It is developing to work at Samhall. I learn new assignments at my own pace and my self-confidence increases for each passing day," says Ylva Hägg. After 26 years working at Ericsson, Ylva lost her job in conjunction with a company restructuring. This was followed by a period of unemployment that almost broke her spirit. It was awful. "In the end, I would hardly dare to venture out. You feel so worthless," she sums up. Ylva Hägg is 46 years of age and believes she has been given a new chance in working life thanks to her employment at Samhall.

In another article in one of Samhall's recent annual reports, one of the employees thought that the kind of work Samhall offers the occupationally disabled was unique. The man compared it with his previous job at a private sawmill:

> "The stress there made me ill." After many years' piecework in the forest, Jan already had problems with his back. However, stress gave rise to high blood pressure and diabetes. – "It just got too much for me. Now, however, I am at the very best of work places, interesting assignments and great management."

Another employee expressed his gratitude for being able to:

> work at my own pace. I have had a few heart attacks. I am not allowed to feel stressed. Previously, I worked for a good delivery company, but I wouldn't be able to cope with that today. Personally, for me, it is important to have a job, even

during the last years of my active working life. I wouldn't be able to stand the alternative of life as a disability pensioner. I need work routines, and especially my workmates at Samhall.

Overall, employees at Samhall explain in Samhall publications that their employment means a lot to them personally, and does not merely signify an opportunity to earn a regular income. One report in the staff magazine featured the story of a man suffering from hydrocephalus who felt victimized outside of Samhall. He said:

"Finally, I feel accepted at work." What Benny has always experienced as being very tiresome is other people staring at him. "People are often so impolite. Many people just stare and then I feel that I really do look different. I've not experienced anything like that at Samhall and I think that is a great relief." He goes on to say, "Samhall is the first work place where I feel that I am completely accepted. Nobody teases me about my disability. I can work in a way that suits me."

In another report, under the heading "At Samhall, Gull does not have to feel ashamed any more," a woman interviewee relates:

I am now 62 and I believe that my dyslexia has partly ruined my life. I attended elementary school for seven years, in a remedial class. When I finished, I had a BD grade, the lowest in all subjects. They said I was stupid, and finally I came to believe that myself also. My difficulties with reading and writing have given me poor self-confidence. I've worked at Samhall for eight years, and here you don't have to feel ashamed of your disability.

In accordance with this picture, Samhall's publications usually contain many photos of smiling and happy occupationally disabled employees.

A Theory on Developing Disabled People

One of Samhall's publications maintains that Samhall has "peak competence" when it comes to the development of occupationally disabled employees, since "work on personnel development is the core of Samhall's activities." At the foundation of this development are some ideas, concepts and theories about 'learning,' 'rehabilitation' and 'the organization of work.' Occupationally disabled people within Samhall are assessed on their ability to carry out a given job based on the personnel development concepts for occupationally disabled persons that have been developed, which is interpreted as "activating development." This idea is taken forward in "Samhall's vision of the future" from 2003, "The right to work for the functionally disabled," as well as in a CEO's commentary in one of the annual reports with the headline "Defend the right to work!" This basis for values within Samhall – that participation in productive work is a "legal and moral right" – also states that a job within Samhall should not only aim to provide financial support, but must also function as an engine for personal development. In other words, the fact that the occupationally disabled employees take part in the businesslike production that Samhall has to offer is the best mechanism for their personal development, which thus emphasizes the legitimate role that Samhall believes it has in society to help the occupationally disabled.

During recent years, 'activation' within Samhall has more frequently come to be translated to 'personal development,' and the origins of this were presented in the document *The Developing Work Place: A Conceptual Document about an Organization of Work*, which pointed out that in time, "obligatory work to earn a meager living has been replaced by *professional* and *personal development* in work, meaningful, independent and stimulating work assignment as well as a professional role that is compatible with a desired future." The document goes on to say:

> even the contemporary view of work has changed during this period, and authoritarian patterns with one-sided demands on the individual's subjection and submissiveness have been replaced by *humanistic values*, so that work should not only be free of risk and pleasant, but should even be seen as an opportunity for fellowship and meaning as well as for the personal development and individual self-expression.

The Developing Work Place, abbreviated to "DWP" within Samhall, is a central theory for activation, and can be found in much of the literature. DWP is even specified as a standard for a method of working within Samhall in the collective agreement that has been entered into with labor organizations, where, according to the DWP concept, the ability of the individual to develop as an occupationally disabled employee can affect his or her wage development.

More specifically, the DWP personnel development concept set out in *The Developing Work Place* policy statement involves the following ideas:

- Active and conscious attention should be directed to composition of the work group, so that a complementary group is formed. As far as possible, the group should be based on difference in age, gender, disability, nationality, professional skills, experience and so on. By virtue of the different backgrounds of the individuals, natural conditions for broad competence in the work team are created, where, in addition to responsibility for the production, it should be possible for a social commitment to develop.
- The size of the work team should be adapted according to the needs within the different production areas. It may be possible for the smaller work team to create positive social effects. However, in the somewhat larger groups it may be possible to successfully tackle absence, training, transitions and

so on without disrupting production. From experience, an effective group consists of six to ten people, but naturally, the size of the group must vary depending on local conditions.

- There is a need for a broad and enriching work content for the entire work team, so that the work situation really promotes meaning and personal development. It should be possible for the work team to take over some of the support and service assignments such as technical maintenance, transport and, inspection, and as far as possible take responsibility for the production of the finished component/product.
- Learning by doing should be a natural thing in the daily work situation. Learning in practical work situations enables individual development and stimulates increased responsibility.
- Work teams should be given more responsibility for production goals. This is accomplished by having the group take part when setting up production, when selecting production methods and in other problem-solving tasks.
- There should be planned job rotation within the group, to broaden personal and group competence and to prevent monotony, both in physical and mental terms.
- There should be a post of group representative that does not imply an extra level in the organization's hierarchy, but which leads to increased learning for everyone in the group and should thus naturally rotate between the group members.

According to the policy statement, DWP's developing effects on the occupationally disabled should be built up "from a lowest of a highest level," which means that employment at Samhall should primarily provide a basic living, and subsequently be followed by "social continuity, interesting work, healing, competence development, transition or continuing work within Samhall in the same level with personal potential." According to the same document, DWP organizes the occupationally disabled so that they:

> function in a context that provides meaning, support and stimulation from other people and social training that leads to a significant improvement in the quality of life, even if the job itself does not offer much in the way of development or stimulation. Fellowship is particularly important for people with social and mental difficulties, but even the motor-disabled risk being isolated without a job. Via an interesting job, it is possible to build further on positive job motivation. Work itself has a value for the individual and provides satisfaction. Carrying out an interesting and meaningful job also provides positive contributions to an individual's self-esteem and intrinsic value. If specialist measures from the corporate health service and 'everyday therapeutic' efforts from fellow workers and management are added to this, it is possible to create conditions for healing 'mental wounds' often caused by an occupational disability, resulting consequently in a healing of the individual.

In this context, a leading official within Samhall emphasized: "Our task is to heal disabled people."

The introduction of DWP at Samhall was a response to generally unsatisfactory working conditions in Swedish industry, which was said to be characterized by repetitive, monotonous and meaningless work operations. *The Developing Work Place* emphasizes: "The mass production philosophy of industrial society was productive, but psycho-socially unsatisfactory. Above all, the needs of the large number of employees for fellowship, professional pride, job satisfaction and personal development were not satisfied." Thus, when DWP was developed, it was decided to implement it within Samhall to contribute towards "a total reappraisal of the 'mechanical' organization philosophy" to create "better environments to satisfy not only human but also technological and economic requirements." Those thoughts and ideas that were summarized in the document were said to be "innovative" among companies in general by constituting:

> more than instruments for such things as increased efficacy and personal development. They represent a philosophy that signifies a break with previous approaches to organizations and people. A production-oriented tradition is replaced by a business-oriented tradition, but based on the fact that work should be meaningful and stimulating for the individual.

A former Samhall CEO wrote in a book published by Samhall:

> In its own way, a Samhall factory can be said to be an ideal work place. Instead of looking upon the occupational disability as a problem, we see the individual possibilities of our employees. Using this approach, it is possible to find a suitable work arrangement even where grave occupational disabilities are concerned; of not looking at a person's problems but of his or her possibilities. When it comes to creating a positive and humane environment at work places characterized by different problems, Samhall should have a good deal to give to trade and industry. In substance, we employ support measures and work methods that are interesting even outside of Samhall.

In another book commissioned by Samhall, the author wrote: "Even from an international perspective, Samhall's knowledge and experience is impressive when it comes to how the company adapts its psycho-social work environment so that the rehabilitating function of the work place is maximized." In a memo, the Samhall CEO of the time wrote:

> A long-term goal should even be an ambition for the Samhall Group to become a model for other industrial and service companies with respect to the organization of work. A model where the organization of work enables the utilization of each individual's professional and personal prerequisites as well as their interest for

development, co-determination and responsibility with respect to the goals of and the means for production.

Learning by Doing

A central point of departure in the development of occupationally disabled employees at Samhall is that activation should take place through practical training, which also applies to all types of formal education. This starting point is based on a belief that occupationally disabled people find it easier to learn by doing rather than through complicated literature studies and similar theorizing. For example, at one work place significant training measures were carried out among the personnel who would be working on cleaning and certain care assignments in municipal homes for the elderly. Materials provided to other personnel in the homes for the elderly (who were employed by the local authority) and to the relatives of those living there provided reassurance that Samhall employees had been trained for three years in dealing with "care situations" with the assistance of a psychologist hired from a company offering a "practically oriented" training course, which would guarantee that the occupationally disabled employees would carry out their work in a satisfactory manner.

A supervisor pointed out that this training, like other training for occupationally disabled people, could not be based on individual literature studies, but instead had to be based on "doing things together." She stressed: "The occupationally disabled would definitely not be able to manage theoretical training, for example the nursing program and senior high school. We have to take that into consideration." An occupationally disabled employee declared that he had not been able to study to become a cook since he "could not pass the theory part." Instead, he now worked in one of Samhall's large-scale kitchens, where "no course in theory is necessary to be able to work." Several young men working at one of Samhall's industrial facilities said that they worked at Samhall since they were not able to cope with school because of their dyslexia, and several employees at another work site had no driving licenses since they were unable to pass the theoretical exam. One supervisor believed, "You can't use writing to teach our employees anything. *Doing* is what is important – practical things all the time, doing things." Taking it for granted that employees are incapable of theoretical studies is in line with a conception of the occupationally disabled as having a low level of education and of being intellectually "weak" in other ways. Thus, practically oriented training courses that are adapted to the characteristics of occupationally disabled people are preferred.

For these reasons, "concrete development on the shop floor" is utilized and "good personnel development develops in daily work," a local manager at a work site explained. A supervisor pointed out: "In order to be able to work on personnel development, we must have something to put into the hands of the occupationally disabled." These notions are in accord with the concept that Samhall offers "development in daily work," which is expressed in several writings about Samhall, for example in various information brochures, annual reports and books such as *Rehabilitation through Work* and *The Healing Force of Work*. For example, *The Healing Force of Work* establishes that "the primary task of Samhall is to develop people," and that "the specific thing with Samhall is that the disabled are rehabilitated through work."

In a presentation about Samhall, it was pointed out:

> A job at Samhall provides an opportunity for personal development and vocational rehabilitation as well as learning. The work itself, participation in production, is the basis for personal development. In addition to the daily work, different support actions and training are offered that have importance both for work at Samhall and for our employees' prospects in the rest of the labor market. By operating a business enterprise, Samhall creates work that gives employees opportunities to develop their capacity for working based on individual prerequisites. That is Samhall's way of working with personnel development.

One of the annual reports states: "For employees with an occupational disability it is 'the job,' participation in production, that is the basis for personal development." Based on this perspective, Samhall is "for people who will strengthen their ability to satisfy the demands of working life via concrete work situations and thus improve or retain their employability," as stated in one publication. One supervisor interviewed in a government study pointed out:

> All the work we do here each day is rehabilitation. It would take hours to give an account of the measures we employ to rehabilitate our occupationally disabled employees. There are as many different methods and strategies as there are people here. That is one of the points of our activities, of adapting ourselves to the individuals. For one person, rehabilitation is learning to get up in the morning in order to go to work. For another person, rehabilitation is not having to sit alone at home day and day out. For a third person, rehabilitation is learning to work in the same team as women, despite the fact that due to his cultural background he feels that women should know their place. Do you understand? One cannot say that rehabilitation is brought about by this or that. Everything we do here is rehabilitation and we work with this in everything we do.

In this context, a government study in which supervisors at Samhall were interviewed concluded that "a common result from the interviews with supervisors is that these feel that the rehabilitation that takes place at Samhall occurs in the daily work situation."

Chapter 3
Identifying the Needy

Normally, employment as an occupationally disabled person at Samhall takes place through the auspices of the National Employment Office (NEO). The NEO as part of Swedish governmental labor market policy has existed since 1948, and caters for people who have difficulty obtaining or retaining work. The primary task for the NEO, as formulated by parliament, and the one that is normally understood to be its overriding duty, is to match people who are deemed to be applying for work with the needs of employers – to help people with problems to obtain employment in a company or similar organization. Many people make valiant attempts to find work themselves, but many – probably even the majority – eventually register with the NEO and are thus formally categorized as unemployed. Applying for work does not mean that one can manage without financial income in the form of unemployment benefits or similar, so these are granted to those who have registered as applicants for work with the NEO.

The NEO has a so-called "assignment right" to Samhall, which means that it has the right to refer anyone applying for work to a position within Samhall. According to the latest government study on Samhall, the assignment right is "a term within labor market policy, which implies that the National Employment Office proposes the person assigned be a part of a labor market policy program or effort." This right is included as a rule in the collective agreement for Samhall employees. However, as will be discussed below, employment at Samhall is based on collaboration between the NEO and Samhall, where the organizations agree that a person should begin working in the company, either as occupationally disabled or not.

Selecting Candidates for Activation Programs

Before reporting on the recruitment program to Samhall, it may be relevant to mention something about those the NEO judges to be potential candidates for an assignment there. Among other things, this assessment should be based on Government Ordinance No. 2000:630 on "special measures for persons with an occupational disability." The target group for work at Samhall is those "whose work capacity is so reduced that he or she cannot obtain other work," as expressed in a government study. An administrative official at the NEO related that employment at Samhall is often preceded by "quite a few trial periods and the realization that the employer will not accept this person, who is too frail, with insufficient language skills, and too much of a question mark for us for that matter."

Another administrative official said:

> When we sit discussing cases with colleagues, we can say that 'this is a typical
> Samhall case' and then everybody in the group understands. It's a kind of
> intuition. We've made enough attempts, and the person applying for work makes
> no demands either, he is just happy to get a job, and so he can have this kind of
> employment. He doesn't care if he sits down assembling Christmas tree stands
> for the rest of his life or works on some kind of assembly line.

A third administrative official was of the opinion that in order to be considered for employment at Samhall, it may "not only be due to a medical problem, but also be about how people function socially, personality-wise, that they need a much more distinct and stronger labor management to be able to cope with their work tasks, and then Samhall comes to mind."

Fundamental to the ideas about occupational disability is the fact that the person applying for work has a number of personal problems that are termed functional disorders: "A person is occupationally disabled if a functional disorder impairs or prevents participation in working life," as a government report says. If someone has problems with sight or hearing, if he or she has lost one leg or both, or arms and hands, has hydrocephalus or other physical conditions, or if he or she behaves in a manner that the NEO recognizes as "DAMP," "ADHD," "suffering from cerebral palsy" or similar "typical cases," there is no reason for the organization not to assume that the person will have difficulty on the regular labor market.

These "obvious cases," as an administrative official called them, consist of those who can often submit written documentation supporting their problem, such as statements from a doctor, statements from special schools and certificates from counselors, where other experts have judged them to be functionally disabled in roughly the same way as the administrative official is now doing. In other cases, it becomes apparent to the administrative official that the person has or can be expected to have problems when he or she "has been referred here from the prison and probation service, the social services or regional social insurance office," as one administrative official put it, and where the person's previous involvement with these organizations is taken as evidence that the person is socially problematic.

For the individual administrative official, the difficulties that are regarded as being prevalent in the occupationally disabled can serve as a basis for explaining why a certain person applying for work has difficulty in getting or keeping a job and needs to be activated in order to become more employable. The administrative official's view that the occupationally disabled have additional difficulties on the labor market is supported by government studies and reports. One of these states: "Recent years have entailed an increase in pressure for transformation, where labor-intensive companies and subsequently even public service activities have tightened up their organizations with more technological solutions and fewer jobs. The organizations have also become 'slimmer' or 'leaner,'" and this has affected the group of "people with functional disorders" in particular.

One administrative official at the NEO explained:

> The requirements of employers have increased all the time, but the people who apply for work with us remain, they are linguistically weak, they are the middle-aged and older people who generally have a weaker position on the labor market. They are hopelessly out of it, they don't have a chance of asserting themselves. Sweden has accepted an enormous amount of refugees, often these have a very poor basic education, many are illiterate and have worked within agriculture in their home countries, and that is all the difference in the world. Here we let our most simple industrial jobs disappear abroad, and the more qualified for that matter. Soon there won't be that many factories left.

A government study observed: "It can be said that the persons in the study [the occupationally disabled] will always be 'at the rear of the line in working life.' This means that this group often is pushed back even further when other groups are affected by problems in the labor market." Another study emphasized: "During the 1990s, the labor market has deteriorated appreciably. This development has a negative effect on the competitiveness [for the number of vacant jobs] of the occupationally disabled." In this connection, one NEO administrative official observed that "the labor market was so much simpler in the 1970s, there were much more unqualified jobs. Those days are gone forever." Another administrative official reported similar experiences in his fruitless efforts to obtain work for certain categories of the unemployed: "It can be an immigrant who has been working as a cleaner for a number of years, has four years of schooling in his home country, speaks very bad Swedish. What do we do with this kind of person when employers can pick and choose?" This administrative official related that in conversations with employers, he has often been confronted with the attitude, "We want the best, we don't accept second-raters."

In many cases, there is no doubt that a jobseeker will be difficult to place on the labor market, based on the experiences of the NEO as these are interpreted by their advocates. However, there are certain cases, the "gray zone" cases as they are called within the NEO, that are more ambivalent. One of the administrative officials defined them as "complex cases, psychologically deviant personalities, hidden addiction, odd customers in general terms," and another official emphasized that they are "people who you cannot point out as having anything physically or mentally wrong, but there is still some kind of handicap at the basis of their behavior." Yet another administrative official implied that for this group:

> one cannot say they have a medical functional disorder, but that there are other causes and reasons. We all have our own different personalities; one can be odd in different ways. One can have deficiencies in one's social ability, creating difficulties on the labor market resulting in long-term unemployment; it is our way of meeting with this type of job applicant where one cannot automatically point to a disorder.

One of his colleagues observed that this could often apply to immigrants, and explained that difficulties with language, which according to him affect most immigrants, have never been an official reason for recruitment to Samhall, but that "language can be one reason why in reality an applicant is seen as occupationally disabled."

The usual method for an administrative official to obtain confirmation of the difficulties of a "gray-zone case" is an in-depth investigation: "If you [the administrative official] are uncertain of the extent of the disorder, you should call in an expert, for example a doctor, a psychologist or counselor," the organization's training materials state. Thus, some of the problematic job applicants are passed on internally to special units. In contrast to the service provided by the ordinary offices of the NEO, the special units have more all-round competence in inquiry issues, which is considered to be especially important for those suspected of having an occupational disability, who may consequently require activation. According to a document about these units within the NEO, in general their clients are:

> people who are irresolute when it comes to choice of profession, the so-called vocationally unsure, or they who feel uncertain in the face of (re-)entry into working life. However, a considerable number of those looking for work have limited working capacity as a result of an occupational disability or other problems with adjustment.

An information brochure published by the Coordination Committee for the National Association for Disabled Persons (a general lobbying organization for various associations for the disabled which has approximately 500,000 members), features a report that the special units have good resources for the occupationally disabled, and offer not only guidance, but also so-called "work-oriented activation."

According to one administrative official, the normal procedure is that the jobseeker initially makes contact with one of the ordinary National Employment Offices, and the official there then refers that person to a special unit. An administrative official at a special unit explained that very difficult cases that the ordinary National Employment Offices are not able to handle "are referred to us, so-called gray-zone areas, cases for investigation." Another official at one of these units pointed out that they had "very good resources" for identifying, mapping and analyzing the personal qualities of the jobseeker as an explanation of his or her problem on the labor market, especially "hidden disabilities." But even "clear problem cases" are normally referred to the special units:

> As soon as the ordinary National Employment Offices have an applicant that they discover has an occupational disability by virtue of the applicant referring to a skin problem, or why he or she cannot accept certain jobs and so on, they make sure they obtain a doctor's report, and then the case is transferred here.

In this context, one administrative official emphasized that it is the "occupational hindrance" itself that is the important thing, and not a "more or less obvious disability":

> You can have a disability, you can sit in a wheelchair and be a data hacker, be a computer engineer and sitting in a wheelchair is no hindrance in your work, you can fully move your arms and head, however, if you are to work as an assistant nurse and are confined to a wheelchair, the wheelchair is the hindrance. Some illnesses can be occupational hindrances, but all illnesses are not occupational hindrances.

However, this administrative official was of the opinion that normally *everyone* who was thought to be problematic was passed over to the special units, regardless of whether or not there was a special need: "It is very common. Most ordinary National Employment Offices would prefer not to have so much to do with those that have disabilities, but actually this is not a correct way to deal with the issue." Another administrative official related that people are often passed on to a special unit for investigation if they have ever been classified as occupationally disabled earlier in life:

> If people have worked for Samhall earlier in their life, having successfully left the organization for a job on the regular labor market, and then eventually get unemployed, then a common reaction among my colleagues at the ordinary employment offices is, "I see, you've been at Samhall before," and then they automatically send the case to us. If you've been employed at Samhall before, this is a very likely response.

Almost unanimously, administrative officials at AF Rehab reported that their workload had increased, which they believed was the result of several factors. One reason presented was an experience that there were more occupationally disabled people in society, which the administrative officials explained as being the result of a more difficult labor market where many people suffered from physical problems due to "stress" and "burnout." Another reason was to do with the increase in resources the NEO had obtained to enable it to identify the occupationally disabled and others who had difficulty in finding employment. One administrative official explained:

> Nowadays, with computers and the like you can produce information about how long a person has been going to the labor offices, so that this fact is more obvious than it was earlier. Now you can see more clearly that some people have been going to the National Employment Office for a large part of their lives, and thus they have a need for certain measures to be taken. So this group has existed all the time but has become more visible for us. Simply put, we see more

of them thanks to our improved resources for identifying prospective cases for activation.

This conclusion was specified in more detail by a colleague:

> If they have become more visible, it can be found that these persons have a lot of problems physically or otherwise, which hinder them from gaining employment. But this group has not only become more visible, it has also grown in size and this is because of the climate on the labor market due to the way working life has changed.

Another administrative official believed that a third reason why the number of clients at the special units had increased was that those looking for work at ordinary National Employment Offices nowadays must be able to use computers and the Internet to apply for work. If you are unable to do this, you are regarded as a potentially occupationally disabled person and can be passed on to AF Rehab for an investigation: "Naturally, many unemployed people feel confused when they are expected to apply for work through their own efforts," and consequently, it "is obvious that the screening taking place today at ordinary National Employment Offices is quite tough," one administrative official explained.

Thus, any jobseeker has the right to be registered at the special agency for the occupationally disabled, but the whole process is based on those looking for work having certain problems finding a job. One administrative official pointed out:

> Thus, it can be that a depression has been brought on by the state of unemployment, leading to the development of social phobias where self-confidence has reached bottom. People need extra support for they are so far out of it, we have many people here now who are what we term "run down," and some of them are run down as a result of long-term unemployment and need extra interventions.

Screenings and Examinations

The majority of the clients at the special units have a "documented occupational disability" based on a doctor's certificate or other socio-medical enquiry, for example carried out by the "Regional Social Insurance Office, a social district, the prisons and probation service," one administrative official explained. However, officials often feel that these studies are not able to reflect the "real" problems the person is said to suffer from. For this reason, a more work-oriented investigation may also be necessary, to complement the original information about the occupational disability. An administrative official thought that doctors' certificates were seldom sufficient for assigning a jobseeker to Samhall:

I don't believe that people are assigned to Samhall at first sight. It has happened, and sometimes 'referred to Samhall' is written on the doctor's referral. The most common services offered by the special units in this context are 'to make clear the requirements for work' and 'to adapt the work situation.'

During some weeks of investigation at AF Rehab or similar activity within the NEO, the jobseeker goes through a number of stages, such as assessing "ability to concentrate, perseverance, social ability," as one administrative official stated. Another administrative official pointed out that by virtue of their skills in analyzing an occupational disability, they are good at discovering "hidden disabilities" – limitations that previous investigations and conversations have not discovered, such as those by a doctor or administrative official at ordinary National Employment Offices. An administrative official observed: "The largest group was previously the intellectually disabled, for they came directly from special secondary schools. However, the group that is continually on the increase is the group of occupationally disabled persons with mental health problems, and among others those that are called 'specific learning difficulties', DAMP, ADHD, Asperger's" – illnesses which, thanks to developments in methodology, can be discovered more easily than in the past.

A lot of the investigation to establish an occupational disability is based on practical work, where the jobseeker carries out various work operations. One administrative official stated that they had a "practical department where you can use a lathe and do welding. Everyone doesn't need this, but for the group that is selected it can be a very good start." In a document describing the operations of the special units, jobseekers are offered:

> wood, electrical and machine work with exercises in drawing and measuring, office work with computers etc. The aim of the practical occupation experience is, in addition to providing the jobseeker with new experiences and insights, to investigate the prerequisites and suitability of the jobseeker for different methods of work with regard to disability.

During the course of the investigation, there are also opportunities for the jobseekers to have conversations with social workers, psychologists and other experts in order to analyze their backgrounds and determine their current status. One administrative official at a special unit named "Young Handicapped" recounted:

> The staff have special competence within different areas of disability. We have skills in youth issues, in receiving young people where they are, and specifically for those that are disabled. Many perhaps haven't learnt to stand on their own two legs being extremely well taken care of since they were little, perhaps very rightly so.

In addition to this, there are possibilities to purchase work training services from external companies, for example in order to examine a person's capacity for work over approximately one month at a normal work place. Most of the examinations at the special units continue in a group, where the jobseeker together with other potential occupationally disabled persons carry out activities "adapted especially for them," as one officer put it. An employment official thought that one could regard the efforts as:

> a soft start for people to be admitted to a social existence together with others in a similar situation, of acquitting the feeling that 'I'm not alone in feeling frustration about trying to get into the labor market,' 'I'm not alone in having worn out my body as a construction worker,' and this is a very important part of our activities.

In many cases, doctors' examinations, work training, conversations with counselors and sociologists and so on are concerned with obtaining after-the-fact confirmation of the difficulties the administrative official has experienced over a shorter or longer period and which he or she thinks explain why the applicant is difficult to place in the open labor market. One administrative official explained:

> If we are dealing with a personality disorder and nothing has been documented, we can't just enter a disability code [see below]. Normally, it is our industrial psychologist who will carry out an industrial psychological investigation. We also have social advisory officers for those with a social problem, and this is so to speak what we discover.

If an administrative official suspects that a jobseeker does have social problems, he or she may call on specialists who are trained to recognize them, as one refers a person with bad hearing to an ear specialist.

In general, the comprehensive investigation is about "persons with functional disorders being able to take part based on their own ability," as one administrative official at the NEO put it. More specifically, activation of the occupationally disabled must "place the individual in the center," as a man in charge of two government studies about occupational disability said in a radio interview. He continued: "Before people get into different labor market policy programs, a proper survey of personal prerequisites should be carried out; the persons in question should be able to select what they want to do with the rest of their working lives, and society should be there supporting this." The emphasis on the individual at the center is said to help to overcome the feeling among occupationally disabled people that they "have little influence over their rehabilitation process" which a government study from 1999 pointed out. Surveys and analyses of the capabilities and personal qualities of employees depend on the ability of different organizations to identify the limitations and problems of an individual with the aim of establishing the jobseeker's need for social interventions, and in so doing offer 'help to help oneself.'

Coding of Occupational Disability

Supported by various studies or based on documentation from a doctor or other expert, the NEO can eventually establish a disability coding for the individual. The disability coding is a requirement for obtaining employment at Samhall, as well as for eligibility for other labor market policy measures such as wage allowances or other public sheltered employment. For example, this is emphasized in the pamphlet *A Knowledge of Disablement* published by the National Labor Market Board for use by administrative officials at the NEO: "It is important that you code occupational disabilities so that you can offer jobseekers special guidance or the labor market policy programs that are reserved for people with a reduced working capacity." As support for the practical coding procedure, this handbook is recommended as a "crib." The handbook contains a general description of what an occupational disability entails: "The concept of an occupational disability has been created to emphasize that a person with a functional disorder may be occupationally disabled for certain tasks or a certain working environment." It emphasizes that an occupational disability is linked to the ability to obtain and retain a job. Thus, the investigation that every administrative official has to carry out as a basis for the disability coding is intended to "identify which *limitation* the functional disorder signifies in relation to the requirements of working life."

The handbook emphasizes that the disability coding is not only important from the point of view of administration for the NEO, but also for the jobseekers themselves. The coding will mean that they have significantly better chances of obtaining a job through a labor market policy program:

> Work for all is an important part of the labor market policy. In order to give those with an occupational disability the same possibilities as other jobseeker, there is the possibility of setting a disability code. The code allows access to more detailed service and/or access to the labor market policy programs.

In other words, the disability code is a certification that a person is entitled to extra efforts on the part of the state in order to provide assistance on the labor market, which is concretely brought about by the formal labor market policy efforts that are available. In this way, the disability coding is an important mechanism for an economic resource allocation to the NEO, and not least to the special agencies.

In the current handbook, the types of disability that have been established in 14 codes are discussed in more detail, where some of them are of somatic/physiological character and the others are of psycho-social character:

- cardio, vascular/and or lung disease (Code 11);
- childhood deafness (Code 21);
- hearing impairment (Code 22);
- serious visual impairment (Code 31);

- weak-sightedness (Code 32);
- motor handicap requiring mobility aids such as a walking frame or wheelchair (Code 41);
- other motor handicap (Code 42);
- other somatically related occupational disability (Code 51);
- mental occupational disability (Code 61);
- intellectual occupational disability (Code 71);
- social-medical occupational disability (Code 81);
- asthma/allergy/hypersensitivity (Code 91);
- dyslexia/ specific learning difficulties (Code 92);
- acquired brain damage (Code 93).

As of the first half of the year 2000, the number of codes amounted to eight. Codes 91, 92 and 93 are relatively new. Some codes have even been changed. For example, Codes 21 and 22 were previously covered by one code, "hearing impairment/deafness," Code 2. A government study reported that the most common occupational disability is Code 42 (33 percent of the occupationally disabled), which "is defined in very general terms, thus popular as a means for classifying our clients," as one officer said. In a similar vein, Code 51 (16 percent) is also used often, as well as Code 81 (12 percent). According to the training material from the National Labor Market Board referred to above, Code 42 is defined as "occupational limitation caused by changes in the skeleton, ligaments and connective tissue, musculature and nervous system that limit the ability to move," Code 51 as "occupational limitation caused by physical injury or illness that is not attributable to any of the other disability groups" and code 81 as "occupational disability caused by immediate social difficulties and as the result of abuse and/or criminality."

Each type of disability is defined and specified on two to four pages in the handbook, covering a general description of the disability and a discussion about "characteristics and extent." There is even a discussion about "things to think about," to make it easier for the administrative official to recognize the disability based on the available documentation and conversation with the jobseeker. The types of occupational disabilities and the descriptions of these – 'indications' of the occupational disability – enable administrative officials to recognize occupational disabilities in jobseekers through their interaction with them, as well as to help jobseekers to recognize them in themselves by presenting arguments that a disability exists.

For example, Code 31 ("serious visual impairment") is defined as "an occupational limitation due to the lack of usable sight and which is compensated for with the use of other senses. It involves a visual acuity of 0.05 or less or a field of vision that amounts to 10 degrees or less from the center." Under the heading "Characteristics and Extent," it states, among other things: "as *visually impaired* we count persons who have such bad vision that they have difficulty in reading normal writing or orientating themselves in a strange locale with the help of their vision," and that "the visual impairment in itself is no hindrance for work. A visual occupational disability arises in the relationship between the faculty of vision and the requirements of the work." Under the heading "To Think About," it states, among other things, that "people with a visually impaired occupational disability do not constitute a homogenous group. The only thing that connects them is that their occupational hindrance is sight-related." Code 71 ("intellectual occupational disability") is defined as "an occupational limitation caused by limited learning ability resources." These people can be recognized by the fact that they have "difficulty in carrying out assignments due to a deficiency in intellectual capacity," for example by virtue of "insufficient ability for abstract thought" and "a slow ability for processing." In his contact with such people, the administrative official is encouraged to think about "taking time to listen, about speaking by using simple, short sentences, giving one piece of information at a time, speaking in a steady tempo."

The practical procedure of the coding itself should take place in consultation with the jobseeker. However, the process of arriving at a determination of an occupational disability is normally not transparent for the jobseeker. One day, the administrative official will present the jobseeker with a suggestion of a code, which the jobseeker must either accept or not. In substance, the proposal to the occupationally disabled person is an individual decision by the administrative official, even if it was arrived at with the support of colleagues and other experts. Consequently, it is the administrative official's experience of the jobseeker as an occupationally disabled person, not the jobseeker's personal experience as an occupationally disabled person, that is the deciding factor.

Based on 308 "occupationally disabled" files at the NEO, in 2003 a government study suggested that clients were typically classified as occupationally disabled after a relatively long period as unemployed clients of the NEO. In the vast majority of cases, no objective impairment in terms of physical or mental disorder is evident, even though clients are medically classified as disabled. As an illustration of this, the study reproduced the file of how a young woman, Stina, born in 1982, who eventually became classified as occupationally disabled according to Code 42 ("other motor handicap"):

September 23, 2000:
Visits the National Employment Office. Has not completed high school. She is now looking for a job. She wants to work with children.

October 5, 2000:
Visits the National Employment Office.

October 6, 2000:
Visits the National Employment Office. She's been temporarily employed in a shop.

April 16, 2001:

Visits the National Employment Office. Looking for a job as recreation leader. [The National Employment Office decides to pay part of her salary as recreation leader as part of a trainee program.]

May 10, 2001:

She has been accepted as trainee at a rehabilitation agency.

July 10, 2001:

The trainee period ends. Stina asks the rehabilitation agency for employment.

July 15, 2001:

Visits the National Employment Office. She says she wants to learn about computers.

July 22, 2001:

She is granted a course in computing.

August 11, 2001:

Visits the National Employment Office. Stina quits the course in computing. She doesn't feel she's learning anything. A discussion is initiated on finding a new trainee position. She is codified as occupationally disabled Code 42, and accepts this.

Based on the conclusion that Stina is disabled, the NEO grants her a wage allowance of 60 percent of her salary. As a result of this, the rehabilitation agency where she previously worked as a trainee agrees to employ her. In her files, the NEO administrative official justifies the wage allowance in the following way: "The occupational disability suggests that she cannot work as independently as the other recreational leaders." Therefore, it is believed that she suffers from "other motor handicaps" (Code 42).

The disability coding cannot be forced upon the person, and the jobseeker must always confirm it by signing a document in which it is clearly stated that he or she agrees with the coding. This signing verifies the jobseeker's personal responsibility for his or her occupationally disabled state, and that he or she accepts those measures considered necessary, such as employment at Samhall. "You must never set a code without the agreement of the jobseeker. You must always do this together with the jobseeker," an administrative official at the NEO pointed out, and in that respect, "the jobseeker should be in agreement with being registered as an occupationally disabled person," as was stated in a government study. Another government study concluded: "This implies that everyone who is assigned to Samhall should have an occupational disability and personally accept this."

If the jobseeker does not personally regard himself or herself as occupationally disabled, the onus is on the administrative official to convince him or her that he or she has a functional disorder that should be coded as an occupational disability. Normally, the administrative official has documentation from investigations by the NEO, doctors' certificates, referrals from the social welfare service and others to support the argument. For their part, individuals must rely on their own experiences. Unquestionably, the person has difficulty in finding or retaining a job, which is often supported in the investigatory material, or by the simple fact that the individual is long-term unemployed or has moved in and out in various labor market policy programs offered by the NEO. One employment official recounted that he always concentrated on "what the person wants and what the person knows," but that for many groups, "will is often stronger than knowledge." This problem of being unable to recognize one's own problems is common, one administrative official thought, observing: "You have to accept your problems if you are going to go on." He gave the example of a female jobseeker: "She has great difficulty in realizing it. It is probably an experience that all the occupationally disabled have, and which becomes difficult when you realize that you have limitations." Another administrative official recounted that a normal attitude among jobseekers is: "There isn't really anything drastically wrong with me and I want a job like anybody else out there."

One administrative official emphasized:

> In my mind, having self-insight of one's disability is very important. Many of these people are in a really difficult situation, they are isolated, they have never been able to keep their jobs, you must be able to take a look at yourself and ask, "Where am I at now?"

In this context, the investigations the NEO has carried out with respect to the individual, such as practical training for certain activities or discussions with a psychologist, often serve to convince certain individuals that they do indeed have personal problems that require action. Administrative officials at the NEO have access to information which allows them to recognize occupational disability in people who do not necessarily consider themselves occupationally disabled.

However, the reverse can be true. A man who worked as a cook at Samhall recounted that he had applied for work as a cook in restaurants for many years, but had always "been turned down," and that eventually he felt increasingly depressed: "At the National Employment Office, they told me you had to be ill to work at Samhall. I wondered what I would do. Cut my arms? You have to hurt yourself, you have to make yourself ill," he concluded. Finding a job was more important than anything else he could imagine, and over the years he had become convinced that Samhall was his only chance, and without Samhall he would remain unemployed. Finally, the NEO placed him on a waiting list for Samhall. His administrative official then asked him if he felt ill or if he had problems, but when he said he was healthy and felt quite well, she still indicated that he had a disability – namely, that he was overweight. Consequently, he was requested to go to a doctor, who certified that he was overweight, which was the official explanation for his problem. His disability code was "other motor handicap," Code 42.

An NEO administrative official emphasized that "you have to have a medical infirmity, you have to have a diagnosis, but we can't only rely on the basic medical data" for the disability coding. Another administrative official thought that many problems such as "hidden abuse, problems with relationships, problems with cooperation, mentally deviating personalities" are not noticed in doctors' examinations or during an initial discussion with an administrative official. Thus, a period of practice can be of decisive significance for discovering personal problems and for coding the person with an occupational disability. As an employment official, you can even find that the doctors' certificates the jobseekers bring with them or have obtained after initial contact with the NEO provide a poor reflection of the problem scenario experienced by the official. An administrative official pointed out: "We require basic data from a doctor, but doctors perhaps do not have a clear idea of the whole picture. The doctors who are asked to evaluate work capacity have no training for this." Consequently, another administrative official was of the opinion that if "we have a doctor stating that no problems exist, we can be presented with a veritable Catch 22. On these occasions, you must encourage the jobseeker to find another doctor who can be more adequate" – that is, who is willing to accept the agency's definition of the person's alleged problems.

Furthermore, the doctors' certificates that are used as a basis for the disability coding do not always need to reflect the current medical condition of the person, but may describe an older sickness or injury. One administrative official at the NEO explained:

> I must admit that one of the good things with Samhall is that they have not always been so precise in requiring recently documented base data, they have roughly accepted what we have said. They have been generous in that way. For example, I have ready many times that in the County of Norrland [Northern Sweden, where relatively more people are unemployed] if you have been registered for a long time at the National Employment Office, they will turn a blind eye to the disability code. Similar things have happened here in Stockholm, although there have been doctor's report that have been years old.

At the end of the day, an employment official needs to have the ability to interpret the jobseeker's behavior as an indication of one of the 14 types of disability, whether or not this behavior is recognized in direct meetings with the jobseeker or is described in documentation from a doctor, work investigation, trained social worker or other source. In most cases, the ability to make such judgments is based on several years' experience of working as an administrative official for the NEO, where one has been trained to recognize different types of occupationally disabled people.

An employment official exemplified this with the "large group of immigrants," where it has been difficult to put one's finger on why some of them:

> were so incredibly difficult to work with, but we always came to the conclusion that it was most often because they had been in wars in, for example, Iraq. They were suffering from something like post-traumatic symptom, they kind of refused any kind of care. Then we had a lecturer who worked with such issues who explained, and then everything became so much more plausible. I believe that there is a very large proportion of immigrants at Samhall who are suffering from this kind of post-traumatic stress. Many of them deny this, anyway, they don't want to talk about it.

By presenting the difficulties of immigrants in adapting to the conditions of the Swedish labor market as a "post-traumatic symptom," the employment official considered that his previous ambiguous experiences were given a meaning and a context. In a similar way, the jobseekers could be presented with 'evidence' that they had a need for assistance from society, since they were not only unemployed, but occupationally disabled.

As mentioned above, disability coding is an essential process to allow the NEO to offer the special social support measures that employment at Samhall can provide, rather than a method of reflecting the person's actual character as occupationally disabled. After a person has been coded, "he or she may be entitled to some of our services, for example wage allowances and Samhall," said one administrative official. If a disability coding is not implemented before the question of employment at Samhall arises, the official will risk being criticized. "The code must always be used when we are going to apply a measure [wage allowance, Samhall and so on]. A person must not be uncoded, for then our controllers will come and say, 'Naughty, naughty!'", an administrative official at the National Employment Office pointed out. To allow an administrative official to continue working with the jobseeker, it is consequently important to convince the official that the jobseeker does have an occupational disorder and should thus conduct him- or herself in accordance with this. Only when the jobseeker has been classified as an occupationally disabled person can he or she obtain assistance as an occupationally disabled individual. The organizational definition of an occupational disability is used as the initial basis for deciding who among the jobseekers has the right to be recruited to Samhall. Thus, accepting being coded as occupationally disabled in order to be eligible for employment at Samhall (or other labor market policy measures) implies significantly better chances of obtaining support and assistance from the NEO in finding a job. This induced the Swedish National Audit Office of the day to ask whether "there is a conscious striving among jobseekers to become coded as occupationally disabled" – though this question has never been answered.

Naturally, it may be unimportant which of the 14 possible codes is set, not least because the codes themselves are ambiguous. Investigation work where experts have already coded the individual in question may assist the administrative official, as may a clear description that the jobseeker has specific problems that can be equated to a specific code. In cases where someone has been referred from the social welfare service, for instance, to the NEO, it is apparent that "it is then about something socio-medical," said an administrative official at the NEO, and can thus serve as a guide for the official in the coding procedure. However, "it can also be that placement in a disability group is carried out without a medical basis in the form of a doctor's report or psychological study," another administrative official pointed out in a government study.

In this respect, the coding system's "unclear framework of rules" and "subjective basis for forming a judgment" was criticized in a government study. It was observed that "there are often circumstances like long-term unemployment and a relatively high age that can be behind the disability code." The same study established that:

> the majority of the occupationally disabled employees at Samhall have either no or only one functional disorder that has significance for their job. When it comes to the severity of the occupational disability, supervisors at Samhall who were interviewed in the study estimate that approximately 70 percent manage their jobs well and the functional disorders have only a marginal significance in these cases.

Thus, the problems and limitations that the unemployed are said to have, and which one assumes are demonstrated by an inability to obtain or retain a job, do not always comply with the administrative disability codes, as was emphasized in another government study: "Many people who obtained work at Samhall have a complex of problems of medical, social and personal conditions which are not so easy to translate and group as one number in the National Labor Market Board's categories of occupational disabilities." It observed that:

> the codes applied do not always correspond with real occupational disorders. The possibilities of the National Employment Office to make medical assessments are entirely dependent on the doctors' reports. It can be difficult to gain access to these and they can even contain a description of only an injury or an illness for persons with more than one functional disorder.

One employment official explained: "There is a technical issue here, and it concerns setting a code, which can be quite difficult since it doesn't always agree with the person's real limitations." It is certainly often maintained that the group termed "occupationally disabled" in working life is ambiguous, which is discussed, for example, in Statistics Sweden's annual study that was referred to above, and in government studies and other research literature (see, for example, Albrecht et al., 2002; Drake, 1999). Common definitions of an occupational disability, such as those specified by the WHO or in the National Labor Market Board's codes for the occupationally disabled, link together an occupational disability with the concept of functional disorder, and specify motor disorders and visual impairment and so on as functional disorders. Other definitions equate a functional disorder with a temporary or chronic illness and sickness, and refer to burnout, mental problems, stomach ulcers and so forth. In other contexts, long-term unemployment is defined as a functional disorder. A member of Samhall's management declared: "If you have been removed from the labor market for a couple of years, you have a functional disorder, you have become passive, you have acquired a new frame of reference, you have obtained a completely new way of thinking. I think that we could very well define them as our target group."

Based on a study of 20,000 unemployed people that had recently been classified as occupationally disabled, the Swedish Institute for Labor Market Policy Evaluation, a government agency, concluded in a report (see Johansson and Skedinger, 2005) that officials of the National Employment Office "may have incentives for classifying individuals as disabled due to various quantitative targets." The report stressed that:

> there are such targets with the respect to the placement of disabled workers in subsidized jobs as well as regarding the placement of unemployed workers in regular jobs. The latter goal can be more easily achieved by placing individuals with low qualifications in subsidized jobs for disabled workers. A classification as disabled is necessary for access to labor market programs targeted to the disabled, such as subsidized employment and sheltered employment.

If they do not accept the label "disabled," individuals cannot be recruited to Samhall, thus becoming eligible for its activation practices. Hence, if Samhall is to transform you into an able and fully included person in society, you must first be made disabled and excluded by society.

Labor Market Conditions

One Samhall work site manager observed that recruitment to Samhall had links to trading conditions on the rest of the labor market: "Sometimes it has been difficult to get employees to Samhall due to trading conditions, when not so many have been classified as disabled. Then five years pass and suddenly things are reversed and there are very many occupationally disabled." Another Samhall manager recounted that many of the jobseekers at Samhall had "turned round and round in the system" for quite a long time – that is, gone through various labor market policy training programs, been subject to different kinds of interventions – and finally "accept that they have a disability, abuse problem, or whatever may be the case. This was quite common during the mid-1990s, those arriving were new employees then, typically those that had been the victims of rationalizations and needed to get back into the swing of things again."

It is hardly conceivable that the jobseekers themselves want to be coded as disabled, a process over which they lack significant influence. Rather, it is the administrative officials of the NEO who are more disposed to coding jobseekers as occupationally disabled in times or environments where it is difficult to obtain or retain a job. Thus, the government agency Statistics Sweden could observe in its 2003 study, *The Situation of the Functionally Disordered on the Labor Market*, that the sparsely populated County of Norrland had more people with functional disorders than the vibrant County of Stockholm. A government study from the year 2000 pointed out that the County of Norrland had the highest figures for reporting in sick in the country. Naturally, people are not sicker in Norrland than in Stockholm; neither do they have a higher frequency of 'objective' functional disorders that could be the basis of an occupational disability.

Internal statistics from Samhall from the year 2000 show that there are 16.6 Samhall employees per 1,000 inhabitants in the County of Jämtland, which has suffered from large-scale unemployment for many years, as opposed to 2.9 per 1,000 in the County of Stockholm (the average for the nation is 5.6 per 1,000). The fact that the state offers work at Samhall in places with a generally poor labor market is not a new phenomenon – it was also the case even when Samhall was created during the era of sheltered workshops. For example, a government study from 1982 established that:

> the most likely explanation for the relatively high percentage of rehabilitation treatment applicants [that time's designation for the occupationally disabled] in the County of Norrland is the generally speaking less favorable development of the labor market in relation to the rest of the country. This seems to have resulted in difficulties for persons with relatively mild occupational disorders to keep their jobs.

A 1991 government study emphasized:

> the decisive thing is thus that the occupational disability is related to the agreement between the possibilities of the jobseeker and the structure of the surrounding market and the demand for manpower. In theory and possibly even in practice, this entails that a jobseeker can be occupationally disabled in city X but not in city Y. A jobseeker can be occupationally disabled in February but not in June.

The fact that it is the possibility of obtaining or retaining a job that defines an occupational disability, and not a personal condition in the form of an established medically definable functional disorder, has also been the focus of several government studies within this sector:

> Many people, even with extensive functional disorders can manage an individual placement on the regular labor market. By no means all individuals with a

functional disorder are thus occupationally disabled. The occupational disability occurs in a situation when the functional disorder makes participation in working life difficult or impossible.

According to this definition, it is the personal occupational disability that is used to explain a social problem in the form of difficulties obtaining or retaining a job, which can be based on a given physiological condition, linguistic difficulties, generally deviant social behavior or a low level of education. This was emphasized in a government study:

> Even if the situation of the labor market has improved since the mid-1990s, the fact remains that the requirements of the labor market have increased substantially, with regard to both work rate and competence requirements. Generally speaking, persons with occupational disabilities have a lower level of education. The possibilities for persons with occupational disabilities and other groups with a weak position on the labor market being able to obtain a regular job have thus diminished.

From this perspective, a low level of education can generate an occupational disability on the labor market – it is a well-known fact that people with a low standard of education find it difficult to obtain or retain a job in today's society, just as it is primarily the poorly educated who are occupationally disabled according to official statistics. With this interpretation, people with a low standard of education together with other groups of people who have difficulties finding employment – those who are ill, immigrants and so on – risk becoming occupationally disabled, and should thus be the subject of society's activation efforts. The fact that "people with functional disorders have a higher level of unemployment than the population average," as was observed in a government study, therefore comes as no surprise.

Overall, people with occupational disabilities constitute what another government study termed the 'hard to employ.' Therefore, "it seems less appropriate to use the term 'disabled' in discussions about the disabled and the labor market." In other words, the occupationally disabled are in many cases "people who have been in working life for many years, but have been let go due to a shortage of work or illness and as a consequence of this have been unemployed for a long time." It is clear that among those who are designated occupationally disabled, there are many people who have suffered serious illnesses which limit their ability to compete with others on the labor market. However, there are also many who are considered to be occupationally disabled without being impaired in a medical sense, which is the point of departure for two recently completed government studies – for example, immigrants, certain groups of young people and people in sparsely populated areas. One of these studies observed that "people with an immigrant background – especially in metropolitan areas – have been assigned sheltered work at Samhall more as a result of their language difficulties than that they – in a formal sense – have an occupational disability."

In general, it is possible to observe, as was formulated in a government study from 2002, that:

> in a labor market policy context, the decisive question is whether a person is occupationally disabled, that is has a functional impairment that also results in reduced working capacity. However, the extent to which working capacity is impaired cannot only be defined on the basis of the functional disorder, but actually involves the ability to carry out specific assignments.

Thus, it is the possibility of obtaining or retaining a job that is the decisive factor, and not whether or not the person is ill or healthy in a medical sense.

Therefore, the term "occupational disability" should be seen from the point of view of the individual's ability to carry out certain jobs, where the disability itself is the work limitation that is actually experienced. This disability can be medical in nature, but in many cases may be something that the administrative official of the NEO feels has is connected with the social ability of the person, his or her linguistic ability, or other kinds of behavior. For that reason, long-term unemployment can in practice be the reason for a placement at Samhall, especially in sparsely populated areas, where, in many parts of Sweden, Samhall may be the only or the dominant employer. For example, at a site in the County of Dalarna (Mid Sweden), many people working there had previously worked in the mining industry, and even though a majority of them declared that they had pains in their backs and knees, they would probably not have been working at Samhall if the mines had still been open. One supervisor at Samhall in the County of Skåne (Southern Sweden) recounted that many of his employees had been unemployed for a long time, "and eventually they are entitled to work at Samhall."

Accepting Disability Coding

One administrative official at the NEO reported that most jobseekers "have an aversion to being coded ... if it concerns intellectual difficulties, mental occupational disabilities. Very many who need a lot of support have stress-related symptoms, and to be branded with a mental occupational disability code isn't very amusing." The very fact that they have needed help from the NEO may been embarrassing. As one administrative official put it: "Many people who come to the National Employment Office don't want to talk about this." Another administrative official vouched for the fact that there are many who question whether they really "need an allowance" in the form of a wage subsidy or employment at Samhall in order to strengthen their employability. Yet another official explained that some jobseekers think that "it is somewhat unattractive to work at Samhall, generally speaking people are that way that they think it is unattractive to be at Samhall." In this respect, a government study reported: "Coding an occupational disability is a sensitive issue. In itself, the coding can appear disparaging for self-esteem and for the possibilities of mobilizing one's own resources."

Despite these possibly negative implications for self-esteem, most jobseekers agree to be disability coded. One administrative official explained:

> People are pragmatic. It's about being able to pay the rent and buying food, they'll have to accept certain things [such as being labeled as disabled]. They get status, can take out loans, the can get an apartment, it brings with it many positive things to become an employee of Samhall.

A former Samhall employee wrote about Samhall in a book (Aulin, 2001), stating: "The work at Samhall was the worst thing I have ever experienced. But I was forced to work there. I had bought a new house together with my significant other. Now, fortunately I have a disability pension." An existing employee wrote:

> I have tried working in one of Samhall's factories. I felt so incredibly bad there that I would rather take my life than to be stuck there. My goal is to get out into the ordinary labor market. For my own part, thanks to Samhall I have a permanent employment, a stable income and an apartment of my own.

According to a government study, the idea behind Samhall is that "Samhall should be a measure for the occupationally disabled who has the most difficult position on the labor market." From this perspective, being assigned to this last resort on the labor market can appear problematic for a jobseeker, a former press relations officer at Samhall thought:

> Nobody can apply for a job at Samhall. Instead, you are "assigned" to a job there by the National Employment Office. In other words, a socially maladjusted person doesn't even have the right to apply for a job. Somebody else tells him or her that it is best if he or she began working here or there. Anybody who has been excluded form working life on the open labor market, the disabled, is more subject to the arbitrariness of others than anyone else. (Rådahl, 1990: 29)

A person working in Samhall's corporate health service who was a behavioral scientist believed that it could be "destructive" for a person to be coded as occupationally disabled in order to be considered for a Samhall position. She took as an example the many new employees at Samhall who have been offered cleaning jobs on a regular basis (which is a growing business segment for the company). According to her, some people have experienced it as "insulting" as they "don't feel they are worth anything if they are cleaning." She explained that many of the Samhall employees have felt themselves more or less forced to accept a Samhall position despite the fact that they do not really want to work there: "Our employees have to compensate for this by saying, 'At least I have a job.'"

That it is expedient to accept a proposed disability code is made even more clear by observing the formal framework of rules surrounding unemployment benefits. As a jobseeker, you are formally at the disposal of the labor market, and normally receive unemployment benefit. Refusing an assignment for employment at Samhall requiring a disability coding is certainly possible, "but then the National Employment Office usually submits a report to the affected unemployment benefit fund to call into question unemployment benefits," as one government study observed.

Jobseekers usually accept an offer of recruitment to Samhall, even if many experience it as "a real come-down, of being set aside," as one NEO administrative official described it, especially since Samhall is seen "to be the last measure in a chain of measures for the occupationally disabled," according to a government study. Thus, many people experience employment at Samhall as "negative, the last attempt," an NEO administrative official explained. Aulin wrote in his book about Samhall (Aulin, 2001): "I have read about Samhall, about how badly people are treated. I will soon begin there, but NO thanks!! Even if this means that the National Employment Office will exclude me [from unemployment benefits], and life becomes an economic hell."

Chapter 4
Entering Samhall

As mentioned earlier, the National Employment Office has the right to assign someone to employment in Samhall. Thus, Samhall should be able to offer work to all those identified as occupationally disabled. Naturally, people with very varied personal and professional backgrounds work at Samhall. At the same work place or in the same work group at a work place there can be people who have previously never had a job, people who have worked as salaried employees or as laborers, those who lack a higher education or people who have several academic degrees. However, it is not the individual characteristics of people in terms of their ability to speak Swedish, carry out welding operations, be a skilled cook, have experience of project work and so on that control recruitment to the company, but the occupational disabilities that have been identified. Thus, Samhall should be able to offer work to the 14 disability types that the NEO sets out in its coding of jobseekers as occupationally disabled individuals. One employment official at Samhall explained: "Many Samhall jobs are not based on any special training … anybody can begin here." A former cook who worked on completely different assignments at Samhall than in her long professional career in school dining halls stated: "I never imagined that I would be working with this, I hardly knew what a nail looked like."

Administrative officials at the NEO claimed that many jobseekers reacted in a negative way when Samhall was proposed as an appropriate solution to their alleged individual problems of disability. As one of them said:

> 'Is it one of those sheltered workshops?', they ask. 'I will never go to one of those and be with drips and the mentally retarded.' The whole of society is imbued with, 'We don't want to have a sheltered workshop here,' it's a kind of proverbial phrase, it has a bad ring to it to say that.

Another NEO administrative official said that she had discovered that if she or her colleague "supplied information about Samhall in a positive manner, then everything was okay." She believed that the initial negative reactions displayed when Samhall was suggested were a result of preconceived ideas and ignorance about the activities at Samhall.

In addition to providing the occupationally disabled with information about Samhall – in written and spoken form, setting out what Samhall has to offer in terms of developing and rehabilitating work and that the ultimate goal is to provide the occupationally disabled with work on the open labor market – some employment officials usually accompany the occupationally disabled person on visit to a Samhall site that has recruitment needs. These visits can result in mixed impressions, witnessed an NEO administrative official :

> I have been out with young people whose eyes were filled with terror, and actually in my opinion, in situations like that, they don't have to accept employment with Samhall. On the other hand, I have been out with young people who have shouted with joy and thought that this was a dream job and needed such monotonous work assignments.

Consequently, not all occupationally disabled jobseekers are assigned employment at Samhall. An employment official working with Swedish-born, highly educated persons "suffering from depression due to fatigue," as she described them, did not think that Samhall was an option for this group: "It isn't reasonable, dignifying," she said. Traditionally, Samhall has recruited blue-collar workers, and those employees at Samhall who have had a higher education and worked in high-income professions in their previous careers have often been immigrants. However, during recent years, Samhall has attempted to recruit Swedish-born persons with a high level of education that have been on a long-term sickness listing. The supervisor at Samhall for this project stated: "I have met so many educated persons who would have been suitable here." He went on to say that traditionally:

> 98 percent of the work assignments at Samhall have not required any kind of education. However, if we can show that we employ highly educated people who have worked in high-status environments, this will contribute towards making the Samhall brand sound a little more positive, making it easier even for people with a low level of education to come here. The more our brand is strengthened, the easier it will be for *everyone* to take to step over to us.

One supervisor at Samhall, who had worked there since it was founded, emphasized that now Samhall accepts a lot more people than earlier, and thus it is "no longer a Muppet Show," referring to the fact that in the past, primarily so-called "mentally retarded" persons and the motor-impaired were recruited.

An administrative official at the NEO observed that significant underemployment at several Samhall units results in "many people sitting around … doing nothing, and [they] are thus unhappy." Another administrative official explained: "It has to be said that these industrial installations in Samhall are depressing work places. It kind of has the feeling of what the working environment looked like in the 1950s and 1960s. Samhall has not kept up when it comes to the working environment." As an example of this, this official mentioned a study visit to a Samhall unit: "Among other things, they had a garbage sorting system that seemed really shameful. I know that a group of administrative officials here, newly employed here, were on a study visit to this work place and were very upset." Yet another administrative official observed that those at Samhall who are responsible for personnel development seldom have competence befitting their positions: "They have been recruited to work with production. If you have a personnel supervisor who is extremely technically oriented, he has great difficulty in managing the process of supporting this person, of meeting the person and motivating him."

Another administrative official pointed to the high level of people reporting in sick at Samhall as a rather frightening tendency: "If the general public were to find out what the sickness statistics and problems look like at Samhall, many would really begin to wonder about the situation there." For this reason, another administrative official felt that it would be a good thing if the Samhall of the future "could be more like a regular place of work," and not have "this skunk-like environment."

One administrative official emphasized that the personal preferences of the occupationally disabled should decide whether employment at Samhall was appropriate:

> I have been out to places at Samhall where I have been so unpleasantly affected, for example they have garbage sorting where the young people are on an assembly line sorting plastic materials, there are sharp objects, a noisy working environment, filthy and so on. I thought it was a terrible place to work. In the office, we had many discussions about whether we should assign people to a work place that we ourselves are so unpleasantly affected by or couldn't even imagine working there ourselves. However, at the same time, we agreed that we should not apply our own values, and we took every young person who was interested with us so that they could form their own opinion.

Despite these observations, administrative officials usually did not shy away from the possibility of assigning occupationally disabled people to Samhall by referring to the individual's personal decision to accept employment. One administrative official declared: "You see that they are desperate to get a job, training is unrealistic, no other employer wants them because they are odd in some way. For them, the fact that Samhall exists is a great thing." In this connection, Samhall fulfils an important function in Swedish society as a recipient of people the NEO and others have assessed as having special problems on the labor market. An administrative official observed, "I have had very good contact with Samhall and the people there I have been dealing with," and the fact that she had a facility like Samhall she could make use of had made her work easier.

For some jobseekers, Samhall is a satisfactory option from the time it is first discussed. Several of them mentioned how hopeful they felt before their employment at Samhall, not least some of the non-European immigrants. One of them said that he felt pride in knowing that he had gained a position in a state-run Swedish organization. Others were generally relieved to finally find work at all, and thus escape the monotony and the social isolation brought on by unemployment. However, not everybody was happy about their employment there, and some felt that they had been assigned to Samhall for lack of any reasonable alternative. One man reported that he had said to himself: "I will not stay at Samhall."

The Formal Procedure

Before recruitment, the NEO administrative official should have completed a document specifying, among other things, the jobseeker's education, previous jobs and possible support requirements, to provide Samhall with basic information about the occupationally disabled person. "Three-party cooperation" implies that representatives from Samhall and the NEO meet the jobseeker to go through his or her background and to discuss the possibilities of employment at Samhall. Normally, this is preceded by contacts between the NEO administrative official and supervisors at Samhall to establish whether there is a recruitment requirement for a certain occupationally disabled position. An internal Samhall document maintains that:

> The National Employment Office and the Samhall Group have the common commitment to promote the possibilities of work for persons with occupational disabilities, but their areas of responsibility and their roles in this work are different. It is very important that the two organizations have close collaboration and similar way of viewing things if they are to fulfill the mutual commitment in an effective manner.

An administrative official stressed that long-term collaboration between the personnel at the NEO and those at Samhall was important, where "we got to know the contact person at Samhall." This entailed cooperation in "organizing the job" for the occupationally disabled position. A major aspect of this work entails "establishing good contacts, good relations" in order to facilitate smooth and easy recruitment, another NEO administrative official pointed out. It is in the interests of both Samhall, which has need for a certain number of occupationally disabled staff, and the NEO, which is assessed on its ability to find jobseekers work, that the Samhall recruitment process functions in an efficient way where individual NEO officials establish long-term and reliable relationships with supervisors and other managers at Samhall. Each national employment office is arranged according to county, which means that each NEO administrative official has contact with a limited number of Samhall units within the county in question and thus provides a limited "Samhall labor market."

Samhall has the option of refusing an assignment from the NEO with reference to the fact that "the jobseeker should actively be able to function in a labor work organization and take part in a production process," as stated in one Samhall document. One Samhall supervisor explained that the NEO sometimes "tries to dump those that are least equipped on us." Another supervisor thought that "Samhall has a corporate organization that also has to function." Yet another supervisor pointed out that "in our installation we have a need for certain occupational disability groups, for instance we can't have blind people here." An information CD-ROM aimed at Samhall supervisors pointed out that:

> Respect in the collaboration with the National Employment Offices is an important basis for the whole of Samhall's activities. When Samhall offers employment, the conditions and work requirements should be expressed so that they do not exclude the target group [the occupationally disabled]. It must not be about formal merits or an exaggerated list of wishes. The limited work capacity of a jobseeker must not be the basis for the Samhall company refusing someone employment.

Samhall has been criticized in several government studies for its selective approach to recruitment of the occupationally disabled, thus limiting the right of the NEO to refer jobseekers to Samhall. One Samhall supervisor commented on this: "Samhall wants those who only have a slight disability, and the NEO accepts this since it can then say that it has successfully assigned an unemployed person to a job."

A report from the Swedish National Audit Office, based on interviews with NEO administrative officials working on recruitment to Samhall, stated that "officials interviewed at the National Employment Office are of the opinion that it is difficult to uphold the assignment right if Samhall reports that there are no suitable assignments for a certain individual." Primarily, this is due to the fact that, in practical terms, Samhall has "precedence when it comes to interpretation with regard to who can be assigned". Samhall representatives defended their position in the report by stating that if the NEO had an absolute right to assign anybody to Samhall, it would become the NEO's "dumping place" for those who were most difficult to place on the labor market.

The 'most difficult' cases in terms of occupational disability generally do comprise prioritized groups that have greater difficulty obtaining or retaining a job on the ordinary labor market than other occupationally disabled people. An internal Samhall document specifies these groups as (a) mentally ill ("applicants who have not had previous contact with working life due to long-term illness or grave mental health or who have been removed from work for a long period because of their illness"); (b) the mentally retarded ("applicants who have received their elementary education in special schools and/or attended day centers and/or have been the subject of an investigation through special resources at the National Employment Office"), and (c) "persons with more than one functional impairment" ("primarily applicants with motor disorders who have other functional disorders, but it can also apply to other combinations of functional disorders, which together result in a grave impairment of their functionality"). An administrative official at the NEO observed that "Code sixes and sevens – those with a mental occupational disability and weak talents – have priority, as do those with several codes" – those who have been coded with more than one occupational disability.

In a joint NEO/Samhall document, one idea concerning three-party collaboration (between Samhall, the NEO and the jobseeker) is that the occupationally disabled person should feel that he or she can influence the prevailing situation. In this process, it is important that the concept of "the individual at the center" is satisfied, which is an organizational frame of reference between the NEO and Samhall concerning how recruitment to Samhall should take place: "With the individual at the center, employment at Samhall should constitute a positive and goal-oriented opportunity for the jobseeker. This entails that the prerequisites, expectations and needs of the individual for developmental and supportive efforts should serve as a guide during each employment situation."

In order to decide whether or not employment at Samhall is suitable for them, some occupationally disabled people receive verbal information from Samhall representatives at the local branch of the National Employment Office. For example, on one occasion a Samhall representative gathered together a number of disabled jobseekers to tell them about prevailing recruitment requirements, and about the possibilities for personal development offered by Samhall. Written information about Samhall is also handed out to jobseekers, which states, among other things, that Samhall pays contractual wages, that they would have "work assignments that are adapted to your prerequisites" (that is, the occupational disabilities that have been identified), that "a good deal of your development will be realized via learning at work," and that "you can try new work assignments. You will develop your ability to work together with others in the work team and have the possibility of taking extra responsibility." Furthermore, "an important goal for your employment at Samhall is that eventually you will be able to transfer to a job outside Samhall."

Setting the Stage

As is the case with many companies, several of Samhall's work places are located in industrial areas or similar labor-intensive environments, separated from the rest of society. In certain exceptional cases, there is no sign or other indication outside the work places displaying the name "Samhall." However, if the job at Samhall is a staffing assignment on a customer's premises, such a sign is an official requirement, even if Samhall has its own premises there. For instance, approximately thirty Samhall employees worked at a private company in the basement of a large industrial unit, but it was not evident that these premises only housed Samhall employees. In another staffing assignment in a hospital, ten or so Samhall employees worked in their own premises, but there was nothing there that bore witness that this was a Samhall work place. In several cases, the Samhall work places are close to hospital or care institutions, such as a clinic for back injuries or a psychiatric emergency room. One Samhall workshop which carried out packing was located on Institution Road, which, according to a supervisor there, was "an unfortunate name with respect to our employees." Another work place neighbored a psychiatric clinic for young people and a number of other care institutions, which was called "the village of idiots" by those in the surrounding residential district. A newly employed occupationally disabled person at another Samhall work place located in a normal industrial area surrounded by other companies said that she felt uneasy about going there before she began: "When you drive past here, you can see that the people are disabled. Some have difficulty walking. Some use walking frames. I thought that all of them were idiots here."

One supervisor observed: "Many are ashamed that they are working at Samhall. They get off the bus one stop early so as not to reveal where they work. We supervisors probably do that as well. We know what people think of Samhall." In some external work places where Samhall personnel are hired, the Samhall employees choose to dress in their own clothes, despite the fact that they have access to Samhall work clothes. Others do wear Samhall clothes, but rip off the Samhall emblem. One employee explained: "We just want to be like everyone else." At a staffing assignment in a hospital where Samhall employees held various administrative jobs, some of them had chosen to wear white coats like the rest of the hospital personnel in the department. An occupationally disabled person working at one of the Samhall factories related that when she met people she did not know, she said that she was a welder, and "If they then ask more questions, I say that I weld bathroom cabinets," and "More reluctantly, I say that I work at Samhall." One supervisor explained that when he was among friends and colleagues from previous work sites, he experienced that "They look down on me a little now. They are probably wondering why I can't cope with a job in a normal company with normal employees." In this respect, one of the occupationally disabled employees wrote in a book about Samhall (Aulin, 2001): "I have not told anyone except my mother that I am working there, as I know what people who don't know the company think. And I know that I am not the only one avoiding talking about it." Even if most Samhall employees have a basic idea about the company and the working conditions that prevail there, they seldom have a deeper knowledge of the direction of activity, whether it concerns the company as a whole or the individual work place where they are employed: "I didn't know very much about this ... no more than what there is in the newspapers," said one woman. A colleague of hers observed: "I didn't know much, no more than that it was for the sick and the disabled."

To the extent that the general public knows about Samhall, most commonly they have notions about 'a sheltered workshop,' which usually implies something less complicated and less demanding. Consequently, "Samhall" is sometimes used in jargon about disabilities in the media or between people. A common misconception about Samhall that employees have are inadequate because of their occupational disabilities. One story in a regional newspaper concerned the municipally employed personnel at a home designed for the elderly in the city of Härnösand reacting negatively to the news that Samhall personnel would be working there in simple occupations such as laundry, cleaning and dishwashing within the framework for a staffing assignment for the municipality of Härnösand. One of the municipality's personnel commented on this: "If anything, having Samhall here implies more jobs for us. So we must take responsibility for them too."

Several Samhall work sites, especially those located in smaller towns, have invited citizens to "open houses" over the years. One of the occupationally disabled people employed there said that others "are often surprised about the fine things we do," and another employee explained: "We have had open house here to show the general public that we make fine things and that we are not handicapped." Another of the employees thought that these activities were a good way to help "people see that we are normal" and that "we are not sick." One of the occupationally disabled employees commented after an open house: "People think that we just sit doing therapeutic jobs, but when they see that we are a part of real production, they are surprised. Strangely enough, many react by saying, 'It can't be good for you, you who are ill.'"

In spite of the fact that modern Samhall has personnel in staffing assignments such as cleaning and property services with many 'normal' companies and other organizations, these activities are hardly known at all, since Samhall employees often wear their own clothes or the customer's uniform. Samhall also manufactures several well-known quality products that can be found both in private and public environments, and in many cases the company is the market leader. However, commonly these products, as well as the quality goods produced in the many subcontractor assignments Samhall carries out for elite Swedish companies, are not marketed or sold under the Samhall name. An occupationally disabled employee at Samhall who worked at a Samhall plant manufacturing sanitary cabinets which was one of the town's largest employers, with 80 employees, said: "People don't know what we do here. People in town believe that we sit here folding envelopes despite the fact that almost every other person has one of our bathroom cabinets in their homes." An employee wrote in a book about Samhall, under the heading "Samhall's Products are Near to You!": "The problem is that Samhall cannot create a distinct image of itself as the manufacturer of its own products. Without knowing it, you yourself have products around you that come from Samhall."

Sources of Introductory Information

Information about Samhall is communicated to new employees in several ways – from supervisors, from the new co-workers, in written materials and on video. For example, the introduction material distributed to all new employees which is signed and submitted to the unit manager after review points out:

> For most people employment at Samhall means that you are on your way! For many it is a question of being on their way from one work or life situation that has been difficult to a new situation where it is a question of finding oneself again. The means for this can be the work you have now been offered within Samhall and which has been adapted to your own qualifications. Eventually is it also about being on your way within Samhall, about learning more and taking greater responsibility for your own assignments. Working in a stimulating work place where the idea is that you progress from one assignment to another. The time at Samhall will be beneficial and stimulating and you will feel motivated for a new job.

At the introductory training courses that all new Samhall employees have to complete, they are informed about Samhall's fundamental undertaking "of creating meaningful work for the occupationally disabled wherever there is a need," as well the number of employees, who the CEO is, the existing work areas (such as industry and service industries), labor organization within Samhall, the structure of the collective agreement and so on. In line with this activation logic, one message that is communicated at the introductory training courses is that employment at Samhall is temporary – it should culminate in a so-called "transition," where the person eventually leaves the company and finds a job on the open labor market. Several supervisors were of the opinion that it was important that new employees were introduced to the idea that ultimately, the aim of a job at Samhall was that the individual should leave the company. Consequently, several Samhall publications distributed to new employees emphasize, the positive side of a transition, and more often than not it is equated with having achieved the goal of their employment there – obtaining their "degree" from Samhall, as it were. Likewise, employees' obligation to accept the transition goal is also stressed: "The employee is obliged to leave his employment in the event that he/she is offered a job with another employer that he/she has the prerequisites to cope with," as it states in the introductory material.

Another important piece of information imparted to new employees is that they should regard their employment as "real employment," as a leader of an introductory training course put it, and not as a kind of therapeutic job or receipt of subsidies. Among other things, this implies respect for regulated working hours, routines and rules, and so on. Some of these are formally stipulated, not only in Samhall's internal policies, but also in collective agreements between Samhall and labor unions. For example, these emphasize that "The disabled must carry out the assignments that are associated with the job. Work instructions as well as other instructions provided by labor management should be observed." When you come to Samhall as a new employee, you usually receive an information pamphlet in which the basic employment rules are specified (assignments, working hours, times for breaks, and so on). The conditional tenure of a post at Samhall "emphasizes that it is a question of employment, work as well as rehabilitation through this work, instead of a work training facility where the production conditions are of secondary importance," as a government study observed.

Samhall wants to perceive itself as a company like any other, and wants employees to regard themselves just like employees in any other company, with all that this means in terms of rights and obligations toward the employer. Consequently, employees are expected to carry out a certain kind of work to draw their wage – work that is organized and formally regulated, and which is said to activate the individual. One supervisor at Samhall was of the opinion that many of their disabled employees were accustomed to simply "receiving allowances from society." Because of this, "they have been able to develop all kinds of problems," as another supervisor put it, such as poor timekeeping, not knowing how to interact with colleagues at the work place, and so on. By emphasizing the formal aspect of Samhall employment, the company seeks to forestall such behavior and introduce the person in question to more 'normal' (that is, 'active') behavior in the labor market. The emphasis on real jobs within Samhall should be seen as part of the stimulating work environment Samhall wishes to offer. A government study declared:

> The work [at Samhall] should be meaningful, which implies that Samhall should produce goods and services that are in demand in the general market. Thus, it is not about jobs that more or less emphasize therapy or about assignments that have primarily been designed for the purpose of rehabilitation or to provide work training, even if the work has a rehabilitating effect. Another aspect of meaningful work is the working conditions should be as normal as possible.

A third piece of information given to new employees concerns their responsibility for their own development as an occupationally disabled individual, both in and outside the work situation. In a Samhall video for new employees and others, the CEO of the time emphasized that each person in Samhall "must take responsibility" by "*daring* to learn something new, by *daring* to test something new, by *daring* to work together in the small work team, by *daring* to feel one's way with a service job, by *daring* to start one's own business," which was also stressed by three of the employees in the same video, who said that it was important "to try something new," for that was "what life is all about." This theme of 'daring' is developed, and it recurs in several of the informatory actions that employees will encounter during their careers at Samhall and which deal with participating in a range of organizational practices linked by the theme "personal development." These include the practical work that has to be carried out, which, in so far as the individual has accepted his or her occupational disability, constitutes a significant aspect of the rehabilitation, for which the individual is personally responsible.

During their introductory periods, new employees usually also receive information about Samhall's history. One Samhall work site supervisor used to lend a book to new employees which they could take home to read if they so wished. The title of the book was *The Roots of Samhall: From Relief of the Poor to an Industrial Group*, and it was published by Samhall a number of years ago. It provides historical background about the growth of Samhall, and is designed to shed light on the link between present-day Samhall employees and people who in former days had similar problems and difficulties obtaining and retaining a job, as well as to provide background about the ideological development of Samhall. It may give Samhall employees who read it an opportunity to see themselves through the lens of history and to associate their present experiences of personal problems with the experiences of earlier generations suffering similar hardships. The Samhall staff magazine also offers new employees additional historical reflections on Samhall and its links to the attitudes that have traditionally prevailed about occupational disabilities. For example, there was an article with on the theme "from lunatic to functionally disorder," which, using drawings of people screaming and wearing jesters' caps, described developments in the perception of the occupationally disabled over time, and discussed the origins of mental hospitals and the practice of forced sterilization.

This framing of Samhall employees and Samhall in a historical perspective is complemented during the introduction with more up-to-date verbal and written information about the company, among other things in the brochure *Samhall: More than a Job*, which states that Samhall is "unique" thanks to "its ability to offer varying work environments for people with different functional disorders and to allow employees to develop and grow based on their individual requirements," and also points out that "Samhall is a part of the Swedish labor market policy. The goal is to create full employment and to equip jobseekers for the demands of the labor market." Overall, this information constitutes an important aspect of the reality that is presented to new employees, both verbally and in writing. The starting point is that employees *are* occupationally disabled, otherwise they would not be employed at Samhall, and that Samhall is a unique organization adapted just for them. Because they are occupationally disabled, they are also expected to develop as occupationally disabled individuals based on participation in the organizational development practices Samhall offers to people with occupational disabilities.

The "Able" and the "Disabled"

Supervisors and the occupationally disabled make up two distinct personnel groups at Samhall. First and foremost, they usually have different assignments, where the supervisors have oversight and administrative responsibilities. Second, supervisors are not assigned to their jobs at Samhall by the NEO; instead, they apply for them through the usual channels (hence they are referred to as "directly employed" by the organization, and are not regarded as occupationally disabled). In Samhall's annual reports during recent years, there has been a systematic separation between the occupationally disabled employees and their supervisors, for example with regard to information about periods of employment, sick list registration and age distribution. In a similar way, the occupationally disabled and those directly employed are offered different training programs within the company as a result of their different organizational roles and resulting needs.

At the work places, Samhall's supervisors normally have their own offices located in corners of the premises, or are completely separated in a physical sense. For those supervisors with occupationally disabled employees on staffing assignments, their offices are usually grouped together with other supervisors in an administrative center, which can sometimes be situated far away from the groups' work places. At some work places, there is a personnel dining room where supervisors often have their own table, which is normally either located in the middle or in a corner, often by a window. Quite often, there are flowers on the table, which may be lacking on the other tables. At some units, the supervisors choose not to eat or have their coffee in the dining room at all, but take their tray with them to a conference room or some other work room. At other sites, they choose to go out for lunch, as do some of the occupationally disabled employees, but in most cases they do not go together. Furthermore, supervisors hold private meetings dealing with various issues to which the occupationally disabled personnel are not invited. These meetings usually take place in a conference room or a work room. A newly employed supervisor observed that when she wanted to treat people to cake at her work place and welcome all personnel, a "strange atmosphere" spread among the supervisors and the occupationally disabled employees, since they "were not used of being together at all."

This separation between the directly employed personnel (mainly supervisors) and the occupationally disabled employees through their different work-related activities can create a fellowship that transcends the boundaries of the work place. One supervisor related that she and her fellow supervisors from other work places often met and "discussed their difficulties, what it's like to supervise the disabled, to talk about their work situation, to get to know each other." Another supervisor said, "We meet almost every day," and that they had "close contact ... in order to be able to cope with things."

The supervisors generally came from varied backgrounds. Some had worked at Samhall since the company started, and before that within one of the sheltered workshops that formed the basis for Samhall. Others had been recruited over the years, either directly from elementary or senior high school, or from other public or private employers. Some had worked with disabled people in their earlier professional careers, or worked "with people in other ways," as some of them stated. One supervisor said that she had applied to Samhall for the opportunity to work with people "both during my free time and in my role as a leader." A co-worker of hers emphasized: "I have worked with people all of my life. ... I have worked with a large variety of people, from children and the elderly to alcoholics." She declared: "It is very exciting working with people who are outside the normal frequency distribution curve." A former press relations officer at Samhall, wrote in a book:

> My initial spontaneous joy at Samhall was the pleasure of telling everyone how it was possible to take care of and develop occupationally disabled people. Just imagine that there was an activity that was able to create meaningful jobs for those who had been eliminated from an excessively hard working life on the open labor market and which could give them new self-confidence. (Rådahl, 1990: 22)

For some supervisors, Samhall was not their first choice of employment and they did not know about the company before they began work there. This was the case with one supervisor, who said that he "didn't want to work at Samhall." Neither did he want to move from the place where he lived, where Samhall was the largest employer: "Of two evils [unemployment or employment at Samhall], I chose the lesser evil." Samhall's CEO explained: "I didn't apply for a job at Samhall because I had some special feeling for those with functional disorders. I was an economist." One supervisor said that in his previous job outside Samhall, he "burned out," and thus visualized that "Samhall was more humane." Another supervisor thought that the calmer tempo at Samhall was what attracted him, and related how "stressful" it was at his former work place because of "shorter lead times. Everything had to be done quickly," and "there was a prevailing atmosphere of, 'If the job doesn't suit you, there's the door. We can't have a person like you here. You just have to leave.'" One head of a Samhall workshop with approximately 80 employees related how he decided to "jump off the career carousel after a life crisis" and start work at Samhall instead. Another supervisor who had been the CEO of a company had finally told himself: "This is no life for me. I was booked up for a year ahead. I wasn't the one making decisions."

Chapter 5
Preparatory Examinations

Before accepting someone for employment, Samhall requires that they undergo a six- to eight-week trial period at the prospective work place. A Samhall supervisor explained that enabled Samhall to "see what the individual is suitable for" – to decide which assignments the jobseeker should work on at the local work site. At Samhall, the trial period is called "in-depth mapping," and it is aimed at "ensuring that the right target group is recruited," and "it should constitute a complement to the information received from the National Employment Office. The purpose of the mapping is to acquire a broader picture of the individual in order to find suitable opportunities for development within Samhall."

The reason why Samhall stipulates this trial period before confirming employment is that the disabilities that the NEO has observed and confirmed by means of disability coding do not always comply with reality. One supervisor at Samhall declared, "The real problems come to light during the period of practical occupational experience. The codes can conceal many things," and as one of his work colleagues put it: "The facts discovered at the National Employment Office are only the tip of an iceberg. The situation is often much more complex, the difficulties much greater." Another supervisor thought that the NEO staff "seldom write down a proper diagnosis" about the person in the documents appended to the jobseeker's employment application, "at least, not from our perspective. The injuries detected can only be seen during practical work. They are hidden from the National Employment Office."

One supervisor explained that she often asked herself the following question with regard to an occupationally disabled person being considered for employment: "What has this person really applied for, what kind of disorder are we talking about? Many people go to the doctor's for problems with their back when they are really suffering from a psychosis." Another supervisor pointed out that the disability codes specified in the employees' case histories from the NEO "often do not tally," and instead, "real problems crop up once they start work." Yet another supervisor reported a meeting with a jobseeker who:

> was clearly ill, he was schizophrenic, but the National Employment Office had not detected this – you understand, they are very clever at manipulating and taming people. When he was here, we could clearly see that he was ill, but when he was at the doctor's he acted normal. Then he committed a violent act in town, and subsequently the doctor pronounced him sick, and now he is locked up, undergoing treatment – there are a lot of hidden things that doctors and the National Employment Office don't see but we do.

Consequently, one supervisor thought that "sometimes you have to kind of begin from the beginning in order to understand a person's real impairments."

Several supervisors referred to mental illnesses and other problems that were more difficult to diagnose that could "lie just under the surface," as one of them declared, and which had not been revealed by earlier investigations by the NEO. It is assumed that people who say they have problems with their backs, difficulties with language or dyslexia are hiding something more difficult and more complex, such as war phobias among refugees or mental illnesses in certain cases of long-term unemployment. A member of Samhall's corporate management explained: "Many of our employees do not look as if they have a disability, but they have mental, socio-medical problems." One supervisor thought: "Especially among the immigrant group, you find lots of people who talk about how much they know, despite the fact that they don't." However, she observed that this "is quickly revealed when they are put to work."

The in-depth investigation into the previously coded occupational disability at Samhall can reveal other disabilities in addition to those already defined, or show that the disabilities that were previously identified do not constitute any 'real' limitations where there are other much more significant problems. For example, this was described in an internal "visionary document" for Samhall, where it was established that Samhall should focus on an extensive and systematic "mapping" to carry out an in-depth analysis of the occupationally disabled employees. One problem that Samhall discovered was that:

> When mapping Samhall employees in the different job security and restructuring projects … the disability codes that existed at the time of employment do not provide a true picture of the person's actual requirements. After the more in-depth mapping, more codes are available and thus provide a more correct picture of the occupational disability.

This is exemplified by the results of an internal Samhall project which carried out in-depth mapping at Samhall's project in the City of Skellefteå: "Of sixteen people, six were judged to have double and triple disabilities. When assigning people to Samhall, the National Employment Office had indicated a double disability for two persons. Mental illness and motor disabilities were added after more in-depth mapping." Thus, thanks to the in-depth investigation, Samhall's supervisors were able to observe *more* disabilities than before. Consequently, a non-occupationally disabled person classified as occupationally disabled at the NEO and who is labeled with a disability code can be labeled with an additional problem at Samhall because of the discovery of more disabilities.

Overall, the recruitment process to Samhall is set out in internal documents that strive for so-called "quality assurance" – that the occupationally disabled employee should be recruited in accordance with an organized methodology based on specific routines and conceptions about how the occupationally disabled person can be activated. As a result, the recruiting process is different for Samhall's other personnel group, primarily supervisors and other managers at Samhall, who do not have to go through mappings, analyses and health examinations. Recruitment, which is part of Samhall's Quality Assured Personnel Development Process, is governed by several documents describing how recruitment, development and transition should take place so that Samhall can reach its personnel development goals in the best way "through honest and clear direction from a central level down to the local units," as one of Samhall's annual reports formulated it. The idea is that all occupationally disabled employees should be recruited in accordance with the same "quality assured methods."

For example, the documents concerning recruitment practices are directed toward the supervisors with the aim of getting them to act in a specific way – what they should look for in the occupationally disabled person's behavior during the trial period, for instance. One document, *Assessment of Work Requirements*, sets out of a number of factors concentrating on individual problems, limitations and other disabilities that the supervisor can use as a checklist when assessing a jobseeker during the trial period. Based on several parameters and questions, the occupationally disabled individual is requested to pay attention to his or her behavior during the trial period. He or she is given a form and asked to fill it in. This form is presented by saying: "The aim of the mapping is for the company to get to know as much as possible about you in order to be able to find appropriate development possibilities for you within Samhall." The mapping is fed back "to the recruitment manager and is taken up during three-party discussions together with the National Employment Office and forms the basis for your first development plan with us."

Testing and Documentation

In brief, "mapping" during the trial period entails the jobseeker spending time in different work teams in the Samhall unit in question and trying out a variety of work assignments and meeting other occupationally disabled individuals. One supervisor explained: "They are able to try out different work assignments and see if they can manage them, whereupon an assessment is completed." During this period, a supervisor follows the person extremely carefully and also has contact with the group leader in each work team, who provides information about how the person is fitting into the team and how he or she is carrying out the work. The trial period should be documented on an "In-depth Mapping" form, and if employment is offered, should be placed in the case history kept on file at the work place (which has accompanied the jobseeker from the national employment office). Before being offered employment, the person should be given a medical examination by the corporate health service, documented on the "Confirmation of Health Visit for New Employment" form, which is placed together with other documents in the case file after the person has signed it to confirm acceptance of the problems and limitations that have emerged during the examination. A supervisor who had recently received a new employee presented a case history where it was clear that Samhall's corporate health service had observed that the person was sensitive to stress and suffered from heart problems, which the supervisor thought was important information to enable him to be able to place the employee appropriately from the very beginning.

In order to facilitate the supervisor's assessment of the occupationally disabled individual during the trial period, it is important to have insights into any earlier investigations that have been carried out, primarily by the NEO. one supervisor talked about the difficulties he had experienced when such information about a person had not been communicated to him:

> I don't know what I'm dealing with, so I have to try and ferret out what problems they have. I'm always asking myself, "What is he classified as, that is, what is his disability code from the National Employment Office, so that I will know how to deal with him?"

Another supervisor said that for many years she wasn't allowed to "know the background" of jobseekers admitted to Samhall, which made her "wonder many times why they had come here. I didn't always believe that they were disabled." She explained:

> They didn't have to declare their background. If you were an epileptic, you didn't have to reveal that, and so you just stood there. We have to know how we should deal with people. Now it's been a good thing within Samhall that we have had investigations into what types of disabilities people have. Often people themselves are quite forthcoming and tell us what their problems are, and when they come here, their documents tell us what disability code they have been assigned by the National Employment Office.

One supervisor confirmed that access to the information in the NEO's case file provided a "good guide, for then we know how we are to treat people from the very outset. There is information telling me that I can't place the individual at certain sites." According to one supervisor, in that respect, the case file helped the supervisor understand "what the person is not able to handle," which was borne out by the experiences of another supervisor: "I get help to avoid mistakes, for example by asking him [the jobseeker] to read aloud at a meeting and he turns out to be dyslectic." One supervisor explained that it was a good thing to have background information about the jobseeker's problems, for:

> You get an idea of the angle of approach. If he has a problem with alcohol or drugs, he can't work with others who also have similar problems. They have a tendency to gather together and find out that they like alcohol and the like. So it's great to have as much information as possible.

To this extent, it is essential that the supervisor has knowledge of the person's problems in order to be able to perceive new employees 'as occupationally disabled' and to serve as a legitimate starting point for an in-depth study where the baseline is that the person *has* problems, but where all the problems have probably not yet been discovered.

Certain groups of the occupationally disabled are more problematic than others in this respect, due to the fact that they have not been in contact with the NEO or any other welfare organization for a long period before coming to Samhall. This is particularly true with regard to immigrants, who have often not been in Sweden very long. Certainly, they go through the same recruiting procedures at the NEO as others being considered for employment at Samhall. However, in contrast to persons born in Sweden, they may lack long-term documentation from the Regional Social Insurance Office, the social welfare service, the prison and probation service, previous employers and so on. Without comprehensive earlier documentation describing the person's status, supervisors need to have the ability to think about the possible experiences an immigrant may have had and translate these into terms of disability. The thoughts of several supervisors came to revolve around "war and politics." One of them said: "For immigrants, who are coming here more and more, it is exceedingly difficult to obtain any background information. After a time, you get to know things that would have been great to know before you started, for instance traumas from wars." However, for many jobseekers who were born in Sweden, the situation is often the opposite. One of Samhall's industrial nurses explained: "You've been a part of welfare circle for so long, the social welfare authorities know everything about you, everyone knows everything about you."

The investigation during the trial period is finally summarized in a "Competence Profile," where the competence at issue is the person's limitations – the basis for employment, which provides a compilation of the person's disability. One supervisor at Samhall observed:

> Regarding new employees, the first thing you do is go through the persons' data, what is their status, and soon you can see that they can't write, can't read, then you have to steer them toward what you think they can learn. You get to know almost everything if you have completed this competence profile. You can see relatively quickly the answer to, "Where is this person?"

Earlier, no such mapping tools existed, but for some time now these have been standardized methods at Samhall.

Confirming One's Disability

The three-party discussions between the Samhall supervisor, the jobseeker and the NEO administrative official also provide support for the supervisor during the trial period in determining the problem status of the individual. In this context, the fact that the occupationally disabled can maintain that "they are only here because there was no work elsewhere," as one supervisor expressed it – or as an occupationally disabled employee at a Samhall work site wrote in a book (Aulin, 2001), "I feel like I have been cajoled into Samhall. I only have a hearing impairment that I don't notice when I am wearing my hearing aid. I came to Samhall primarily because I was unemployed" – can be regarded as problematic since you cannot officially propose employment at Samhall solely based on unemployment alone. According to one supervisor, in this respect, discussions with the occupationally disabled individual are aimed at "focusing on the disability, especially if it is not a visible disability." In these discussions, it is important that the jobseeker is entirely open about his or her problems: "It is about turning the problems inside out," another supervisor reported, and getting them to "think about and realize why they have ended up here at Samhall."

In that respect, the questions that supervisors at Samhall and NEO administrative officials ask the individual, which are based on the inter-organizational routines established between the NEO and Samhall regarding the recruitment of occupationally disabled people, presuppose that the person *is* occupationally disabled, which he or she has agreed to through a disability coding at the local branch of the National Employment Office. Consequently, any other point of departure for discussions would not be feasible. When the individual finally begins work at a Samhall site in order to try out one or more sub-operations, it is still "important to be open with your problems, for then you are accepted by the work group, otherwise people just go around wondering and there is an uneasy atmosphere," one supervisor explained. Thus, another supervisor used to encourage the occupationally disabled person during the introduction to "Be honest and tell me what's wrong with you!" Anything that has not come out during earlier discussions and practice will come out then, a supervisor emphasized, "especially things like addiction problems that people can often conceal." Furthermore, the introduction procedures may give recruits an idea of how Samhall will look upon them in future. For example, a supervisor asked a person who was on a trial at one of Samhall's work places: "If you think you are so terrific, then why do you think you are here?"

One supervisor explained that many of the jobseekers lack "an insight into their problems" when they come to Samhall: "Many do not realize their limitations, they are often very verbal so they can deceive most people, although they don't know as much as they think they can, which becomes clear pretty quickly … a lot of them have inadequate knowledge of themselves." Another supervisor at a Samhall cleaning unit, who during recent years has received a number of new employees, many because of closures in industrial production, reported: "Many who come here do not think they have any problems, especially not in relation to cleaning work, which they think is common and simple. However, this is not the case. The job is difficult and complex, so obviously they are disabled." Another supervisor explained that "Many have the will, but can't assess what is feasible.

They can't do what they want to do, they don't understand, for example, they can't count or write. It isn't always that easy for them to understand what is happening around them. They have a long way to go." Another supervisor related that some of his personnel "don't understand normal instructions," pointing out a group of so-called "mentally retarded" individuals who sat working at a packaging job. "They don't understand. The point doesn't always go home for them. Such things are normal at a work place, but the most difficult thing for them is realizing that they don't understand."

Another supervisor gave the example of immigrants that had been recruited to Samhall. According to her, many claimed that a poor knowledge of Swedish was the reason for their lack of success in finding a job on the open labor market: "However, often it is something else, for instance something mental. We find out about war issues, phobias, that people get angry without reason, often they are suffering from different kinds of trauma." An information CD-ROM produced by Samhall for its supervisors states:

> The distribution of occupational disabilities among Samhall employees with immigrant backgrounds deviates from the total distribution at Samhall. Motor disabilities, somatic illnesses and hearing impairments are clearly over-represented, while mental and intellectual occupational disabilities are under-represented. We can, however, presume that mental functional disorders are significantly more common than is shown by the distribution of occupational disabilities at Samhall, since mental and physical injuries due to war, persecution, torture and other traumatic experiences occur frequently among refugees.

Determining and diagnosing a picture of the problem in the new employee that he or she will eventually also come to embrace is an important part of the Samhall recruiting process, and is ultimately about establishing requirements for suitable assignments within the company. If an employee "does not know his disability code," as one of the supervisors put it, the supervisor can have problems placing the person "in the right place." One supervisor explained that some occupationally disabled people say, "'There's nothing wrong with me' when they come here. It is easier for us when they have an insight into this at an early stage." Another supervisor gave the example of the visually impaired: "For example, I have worked with blind people. It's about getting them to accept that they have a lot of problems. Many of them do not have a knowledge of their illness when they start with us." A supervisor working with a cleaning unit who had often had to receive many new personnel during recent years related that recruits to Samhall often "say that they are healthy, but they do not understand that they are sick and have problems. They do not understand that they are sick themselves, so how can they then understand that their colleagues are also sick?"

As a result, one supervisor thought it was important for her "to persuade people to understand that they were already disabled before employment became a reality. This self-knowledge is of pivotal importance for the person being able to work for us." A colleague of hers explained: "Many people come here believing that they can manage all kinds of things, but that isn't the case." She thought that this was a result of inadequate self-knowledge, and "is typical for new occupationally disabled employees" – those who have recently received an occupational disability code. Only when individuals have accepted their problems is it possible to assume that they will be able to function well in their jobs at Samhall: "Alcoholics are so clever and industrious in their work when they have realized that they are alcoholics," one supervisor concluded. However, the "lack of self-knowledge" in many jobseekers at Samhall – the reluctance to consider oneself as occupationally disabled – was not always seen as the fault of the persons in question by the supervisors, but also because the NEO was not clear about this. A nurse at Samhall's corporate health service who had carried out health interviews before employment explained: "Now and again we meet people who say, 'I'm not occupationally disabled,' where they are not aware that they have a disability code, and that's something of a shame. The National Employment Office doesn't always tell them what code they have."

On the whole, supervisors at Samhall felt that the company had improved at determining problems and limitations in the form of occupational disability at an early stage, before the person had been employed, not least thanks to the fact that supervisors had been trained to interpret behavior as an indicator of different illnesses or disabilities. One supervisor related that the nationwide training course in disability studies that all supervisors complete had helped her colleagues deal with occupationally disabled persons by helping them understand "how a typical occupationally disabled person can behave." Other supervisors thought that they had grown better at creating a trustful relationship with jobseekers in an effort to induce them to be more open about their problems. One supervisor observed: "Sometimes people are not open about their problems and we only discover over time that they do not know certain things or that they don't understand but just take chances. Thus, it is important that we gain their trust at an early stage."

Attitudes among Managers

Some supervisors at Samhall reported that at the beginning of their careers there, they had felt confused in their meetings with the occupationally disabled employees. However, it had become easier to relate to them after obtaining information about these persons' problems, either from more experienced supervisors about specific personal difficulties in the form of alcoholism, dyslexia, mental illness and so on, or thanks to their own investigations into these personal problems. One supervisor admitted that she "didn't know anything about functional disorders when I came here. It took years to learn about them." Another supervisor explained:

> In the beginning I thought like this: "I won't enquire into their occupational
> disabilities, why they are here," but after a while I discovered that it's initially

better to go through their files to see what kind of occupational disability they have in order to encounter them in a better way.

Samhall's CEO thought that nowadays, "disabilities are not visible" at Samhall compared to earlier, when Samhall primarily employed "the motor-disabled and mentally retarded." The CEO explained: "An addiction is invisible, and consequently many people may think that 'these people are healthy,' and this is clearly a dilemma for us." A member of Samhall's corporate management related his own experiences of a visit to a work place when he was a new employee:

> I was talking to a guy, and then asked a supervisor, "What does he do here?" It was as if I had been talking to someone who was entirely on an equal footing with me. Then the supervisor told me that this was a guy who had been involved in a terrible car accident. He couldn't function properly. We have people like that here, and we should utilize them.

A behavioral scientist who trained Samhall's supervisors in "receiving the disabled" related that she had met many supervisors "who are really bewildered when it comes to dealing with situations," and gave the example of immigrants, where it can be difficult to imagine what they have experienced, and consequently, "They do not know how to treat those who have experienced torture and other things." Thus, at some work places experts were sometimes hired who gave information about different kinds of disabilities, such as epilepsy, social phobias and ADHD, and how these disabilities can be recognized in employees' behavior. One supervisor observed: "We try to learn about disabilities. People come here and inform us, and we go on courses. You have to learn to recognize the symptoms."

In order to "better diagnose disabilities," as one supervisor put it, all supervisors at Samhall complete a training course called "Functional Disorder: A Disability or a Possibility?" According to the course materials, it is intended to help "recently employed supervisors to quickly familiarize themselves with the conditions of those employees with disabilities." An official at the NEO thought that in general, it was important that the staff at Samhall were trained in understanding the disabled, as "some supervisors [are] really frustrated that they cannot handle their personnel." In Samhall's staff magazine which is distributed to all employees, the course was presented as training for the supervisors in "being able to encounter employees with a functional disorder in a more professional way and become more confident in one's professional role" and "increasing the understanding of different functional disorders and the consequences these can have in work and private life. It entails learning more about how we [supervisors] should receive" occupationally disabled employees.

According to the course description, the course aims at "guaranteeing that employees with functional disorders encounter a professional reception" from supervisors and "emphasizing Samhall's profile as a personnel developer of persons with functional disorders." One goal is:

that as a supervisor/manager/support resource within Samhall you are afforded the opportunity to develop a basic knowledge of the most common functional disorders and the aids available to compensate for impaired functions, that you should increase your understanding of those you encounter in your daily work, of their life situation and needs.

In that respect, the course is also aimed at "giving people that have completed the course more confidence in their professional role."

Some supervisors who had completed the course testified to its positive effects: "We have got to know each other during this training course and will continue supporting each other," said one of them in the staff magazine. Another course member thought that knowledge of the problems and limitations of the occupationally disabled had increased. Another supervisor who had also attended the course thought that she had gained a lot of advice on "how to deal with the disabled": "Without these courses, I would have had to get a lot of help," she said. A newly employed supervisor who had never worked with occupationally disabled people before declared that when he came to Samhall, he was "received really well," and was impressed by the comprehensive introductory training courses offered to him and other newly employed supervisors. In contrast to other companies he had worked for, where "the introduction was completed within a matter of hours," several weeks were devoted to "entering into this special world, the world of Samhall." He thought that the courses he attended "straightened out a load of questions regarding the disabled."

Regardless of their reason for employment in Samhall as supervisors, many of them felt that their time at Samhall often involved major changes in their understanding of what an "occupationally disabled employee" was. A supervisor who had previously worked for twenty years in industry thought:

> Eventually, you become adjusted. Initially, it was difficult that things progressed so slowly, but after a while you get into things. … I have become calmer, have reduced my pace. There's no point in stressing, you have to have more long-term planning for everything and not be involved in abrupt changes, for then you upset their [the occupationally disabled personnel's] calculations.

Several supervisors perceived their charges as "obviously disabled" compared to themselves and others, in the sense that they were considered to be medically sick, physically or mentally functionally disordered, or generally deviant, odd and different. During personnel presentations, a number of supervisors presented individuals or groups of individuals from the point of view of their impairment, which was also a normal occurrence in Samhall's staff magazine and other Samhall publications. One supervisor expressed it as, "The personnel force consists of mentally retarded individuals, addicts, the physically disabled," and a newly employed manager at a Samhall work place said: "They [the previous managers] had mixed so many different disabilities here – paralyzed, language difficulties, phobias – and then they expect us to distribute the work and resolve things ourselves." A third supervisor, sitting down with a group of disabled employees eating lunch, introduced several of them with the comments, "The person there is both blind and deaf. He is flat-footed," as well as, "She is dyslectic, has a slight difficulty in understanding."

Some supervisors pointed out that a disability code was a requirement for employment at Samhall, thus it was only logical to regard employees as "disabled." A fellow worker clarified: "Employment at Samhall is based on the fact that you *have* a disability, a sickness or a problem." As a result, another supervisor thought that if a person was employed at Samhall, this was "evidence" that there were problems, so: "The question about what is wrong with you is 'in the air.'" This opinion was shared by a supervisor at another work place, who said: "All those working at Samhall have problems. That's why they are here."

One supervisor who had worked at Samhall for seventeen years and was interviewed in the staff magazine observed: "Usually, most people who come to us have a fairly complicated work history." Another supervisor thought: "Perhaps some of our employees aren't that talkative; perhaps they are a little surly, somewhat troublesome, and this can be a criterion for starting to work at Samhall." Yet another supervisor said: "Many who come here have had breakdowns," possibly after experiencing "terrible things in war," or "have gone through special schools and been told that they are stupid." One supervisor observed: "The occupationally disabled are so frayed when they come here. Persons at other companies who I have talked with are so impressed, saying, 'How do you cope with all this responsibly resting on your shoulders?'"

The attitudes supervisors have toward the employees as occupationally disabled individuals affect their behavior towards them, because they are aware of the previously established problems and limitations. Meetings and similar gatherings often start with a supervisor asking the question, "How do you feel today?" or similar, and in both writings and speech, the medical-sounding terminology of "psychosocial environment" is sometimes used. A supervisor at a meeting with around thirty occupationally disabled employees declared: "The primary objective for me as a supervisor is that you feel well, that you are happy, that you are having fun. If this works, then all your problems will be resolved. The objective is to develop a good group that feels at home in a good psychosocial environment."

Based on information about the limitations of the employees, one newly employed supervisor of more than seventy employees related:

> The differences here [because of the variety of disabilities] have often made me think, "From a personal point of view, what can this person manage?" – not what he has previous professional training for, but what he can cope with from a medical point of view. I have to see them every day, see how motivated they are. I have to think, "How hard can I proceed?"

He stated that sometimes he happened to say, "You should be able to do this," with the result that:

> She then left crying. Oh well, now I've lost one of my workforce. Now I have zero performance. On the ordinary labor market, if anyone behaves in that way, you simply say, 'The door's over there.' Here, you have to work with a much broader spectrum. I have to work with individuals, talk to them, hold personal development discussions, pursue rehabilitation with them.

Another supervisor witnessed similar experiences: "Of course, you know this. When you work for another company, you take for granted that people can manage things, but not here. Here they are disabled, and I have to accommodate this." A newly employed supervisor at a workshop observed: "Information has another meaning here. At my previous place of work I could inform employees about the state of the market, about order intake. Here, it is the small things that matter – for example, that a light in the parking lot doesn't work."

One supervisor emphasized: "The occupationally disabled do not have to accomplish as much as those working in a workshop down in the town." Another supervisor often had to "apply the brakes on my employees," as he put it, and then turned to one of them working in a storeroom on a staffing assignment: "You won't be able to cope with the stress and the pressure. It's better if you feel okay." A co-worker who was supervisor for a group of about fifteen "workers with low intellect," as he termed them, emphasized: "You can't talk to these people like you can to ordinary workers. You can't be a boor. You have to take it easy. People are very sheltered here. In a normal company, you can push people in a different way." Another supervisor criticized a group leader in a work team at an external employer because he had "loaded too much work" onto two of the occupationally disabled employees in the group: "You have to remember that they are impaired," he concluded. On the whole, several supervisors experienced that "You can't demand as much of them as you can in normal companies," as one of them put it, since "Many of our employees are limited by knowing that they aren't able. They can't see, they can't walk properly, they don't comprehend. They've heard all their lives about what they can't do."

Chapter 6
Finding the Client the Right Place

The investigation of the occupationally disabled person during the introductory period aims to provide a "position adapted to the individual," which is a catchword for Samhall, and is laid down in the company's "fundamental values" as well as in the company's "personnel concept – the individual at the center." A member of Samhall's corporate management declared, "We should create a distinctive image of ourselves as a personnel development company, where people are employed after careful mapping," which was also summarized in a brochure: "The work tempo is adapted according to the individual's requirements. Functional disorders are compensated for by specially designed work environments and work adaptation." The mapping of the individual, both before and during employment, aims to offer an adapted working environment based on the difficulties and problems that he or she is presumed to have on the basis of the occupational disability that has been established.

Notions about a "position adapted to the individual" based on a mapping of employees were summarized by a supervisor as "setting the right person at the right place from the outset, based on his or her disability." To that extent, individual adaptation is based on the type of disability. According to another supervisor, the trial period at Samhall is geared to "ascertaining what the individual can tackle successfully" – for example, "Can he cope with cleaning stairs, can he cope with external property maintenance?" As was mentioned earlier, the suitability of an individual for different types of work at Samhall is based on the person's problems and limitations in terms of occupational disabilities, and not their professional background, education or similar qualifications. Samhall can offer different types of occupations adapted to different groups of disabilities, such as work suitable for the visually impaired, those with motor disabilities and so on.

Thus, Samhall's activities are constructed around the occupational disabilities that the company believes its employees have. If a person has a social phobia, the company does not expose him or her to a lot of people. A visually impaired person can work in a dark room, but not at soldering electronic components, where the faculty of vision is essential. A person with a motor disability is presumed not to be able to work at cleaning stairs. One supervisor related that at his work place, the distribution of work was arranged "on the basis of stress level," where different phases of work were regarded to be stressful in different ways, and that "the stronger ones", as he referred to some of the occupationally disabled workers, could work on more stressful jobs, and "the weaker ones" on less stressful assignments.

Consequently, different work teams usually carry out different tasks based on the disabilities members are said to have, which in concrete terms implies that the existing established occupational disabilities form the basis for the practical placement in a work group. The reason for assigning a new employee to a specific work place may be that he or she has certain established limitations that make that person suitable for the work carried out there, and this division usually continues at the work place in question. If a person is declared to have "a low intellect," he or she will be considered suitable for assignments offered at certain Samhall work places, whereas a woman with an immigrant background who has been a housewife all her life will be offered work on assignments matching this disability. If someone is dyslectic, he or she will be considered for specific assignments at specific work places, and so on.

Certainly, Samhall's personnel come from a variety of personal backgrounds, but as a result of the disability coding established at the national employment office, they are placed in different personnel categories, which make up the work groups deployed to different work places. This division between groups of the disabled, which entails working at different work places or on different tasks within the same work place, is in keeping with the disability-adapted environment that Samhall wishes to achieve, and when the work is group-based, this adaptation will be group-oriented.

A necessary conclusion for disabled employees at Samhall is that their disability is 'their qualification' – the established disability is what justifies their employment at Samhall, and the fact that the individual is considered for certain jobs *for the disabled* makes it reasonable for a supervisor to express: "We have great diversity here. Here, you will find all kinds of disabilities." The designated disability, and not previous experience such a background as a successful dentist, carpenter, cook, metalworker and so on, is what governs the placement of people in work teams and the assignment of work tasks.

In those cases where Samhall has focused on the qualifications of the employee (such as specific professional competence) and not on the disability in recruiting personnel, the company has been criticized. A report from the Swedish National Audit Office objected to the fact that from time to time Samhall had looked for people with "special qualifications rather than persons with special needs" due to an occupational disability. When they are about to identify people with occupational disabilities in order to employ them, Samhall and the NEO's starting points are such qualities as illness, injury and social divergence, not professional skills, experience, creativity and other characteristics that are the usual focus when recruiting and placing people in other organizations.

Matching Disability with an Appropriate Position

The composition of the work groups within Samhall should be based on a "match" between established difficulties and problems in its members and existing and possible jobs, which leads to relatively homogenous work groups made up of such categories as the visibly impaired, alcoholics, the deaf and those confined to wheelchairs. A supervisor who was responsible for external staffing assignments where the personnel at Samhall worked at other companies' premises with personnel that were hired in pointed out that these jobs were more difficult and more demanding than those normally offered at Samhall. For this reason, he thought that the personnel there "are among the better ones at Samhall. We don't have those with the gravest disabilities. They must be able to meet the customers."

In one workshop, a group of deaf employees worked with noisy machines, and at another work site a severely hearing-impaired person worked on spot-welding metal plate, which was also a noisy job. Unlike other personnel, who had difficulty communicating with each other due to the noise, communication between the hearing-impaired workers was no problem, since they used sign language. At another work place, a group of immigrants of Iranian origin were given the task of sorting pension selection forms in preparation for microfilming or scanning for filing. The group spoke Persian, both during work and during coffee breaks. One supervisor thought that the work group functioned "very well." In their homeland, several group members had worked in administrative jobs – for example, in banks or as secretaries – but of a "much more demanding kind," as one of them pointed out. Thus, the appropriateness of the assignment was not due to the fact that the workers had previous experience of office work, but that the work did not require advanced skills in Swedish (which was the unspoken reason why the individuals could not get work in the normal labor market). The work consisted of inspecting and checking forms based on a number of decision rules that stated that an approved form should carry the name in a special box, a cross for the selection of the pension, and a signature, which did not require an ability to read or otherwise communicate in Swedish.

A manager within Samhall working on arranging external trainee jobs for Samhall employees with other employers thought that this behavior of working on assignments appropriate to one's disability at Samhall was problematic:

> For example, when I was out visiting companies within the furniture industry a year ago, the company there required that "You must speak Swedish in the company, no matter where you come from." At Samhall they are grouped according to country and speak their own languages. They isolate themselves, and I believe it will be extremely difficult for them to work for another company.

At a laundry facility, there were three principal work phases that were divided between three work teams: sorting, washing and finishing. A supervisor there explained: "Here, we have the right people in the right place." The sorting group received the dirty washing and sorted it into boxes, where they assigned it a customer number, a color, wash temperature and so on. Another supervisor observed that it was difficult to get people to do this kind of work, since "we sometimes have very deplorable laundry" –dirty or evil-smelling. The work pace was calm and peaceful, and the group worked conscientiously to ensure that no laundry was incorrectly sorted, which would create problems in the subsequent work phases. The group consisted of people who "want peace and quiet," said one of its members. She explained that she did not get on well when stressed or rushed, which had led to "things not working out well in other jobs." Another person explained that he did not feel comfortable in situations where he "didn't know what to do." Thanks to the strict organization of the work based on customer number, color and wash temperature that dictated into which boxes the dirty laundry was sorted, he felt that there was "order" here: "It's working out well here, the job suits my problems."

In the laundry room itself, which consisted of a whitewashed space without windows where 15 washing machines and 10 tumble-dryers were lined up above a number of drying cabinets, there was a lot of bustle. The radio was always playing, the music filled the room, and some of the employees disappeared in whirls of dance, and embraces and kisses were even exchanged. One supervisor apologized for it all, saying, "They are mentally retarded," but was pleased with the "childlike and amusing atmosphere" that prevailed. The main phases of the work involved loading and unloading the machines, which the employees took care of meticulously by going back and forth, carefully monitoring which machine was about to finish its cycle. The machines were going all the time, and there was always some machine that needed to be filled, which took place immediately when there was laundry available. The detergent was filled automatically via tubes from a container into the machines, and the wash temperature was set by one of the supervisors, so the employees could concentrate on their laundry tasks of filling and emptying machines.

On one occasion, Swedish Radio carried a story from this Samhall work place, where one of the employees in the laundry group who was introduced as "mentally retarded" related, "I have one like that [washing machine] at home, it isn't so difficult." One of the supervisors added:

> We all have an important role to fill. You have an important role. Someone has to do it, and you do it very well. Just the fact that you come here every day, you are almost never sick. It is terribly important for me as a supervisor to know, 'Do we have enough people in the laundry?' without you here, and you are so damn good at what you do.

The reporter concluded: "While we are talking, Sven Johansson [the disabled employee] is looking after 14 machines and is ready to step in as soon as anything stops."

The reporter hinted that the work was monotonous and repetitive, but a member of Samhall's corporate management who was also was interviewed for the radio program did not agree:

> He worked for ten years, was out in industry, and when he got assignments, they were simple and monotonous. He has come in here and actually has an important role in the whole of this work process. Here, you see the difference:

this type of work, it varies a lot more, you can set it up, do it in a different way, it isn't as monotonous as it often can be if you are out working in industry. Most importantly, however, this job fits his disability.

The third work phase in the laundry facility was called "finishing," and mainly involved mangling and ironing the laundry, then sorting it for transport to the customer. Approximately twenty women and one man worked there. Of these twenty or so employees, three or four had Swedish as their mother tongue. The majority of them had previously either been housewives in their former home countries and then busied themselves with domestic chores, for example in the form of ironing and mangling, or worked in the now discontinued Samhall textile and clothing industry. In this case, their 'disability,' primarily having done "housework" (which was the most likely cause for them having such difficulty in finding jobs on the open market), constituted their qualification to be at Samhall: there was a great need for people who were good at ironing and mangling, and these people definitely fitted this category. Thus, the assignments fitted these ex-housewives like a glove: "These are the same jobs as they do at home," one of them explained.

This placement based on the type of occupational disability that prevails within Samhall work places is also found in the different units within the company which are directed towards a variety of activities, such as cleaning, elder care, carpentry, riding schools, farms, restaurants, hotels, large-scale kitchens, mechanical workshops and so on. The name of the work group or work place indicates the disabilities that the employees are perceived to have – for example, the general feeling within the company was that packaging was among the simplest and most basic jobs that existed, and that only "people with minimal talents and those otherwise limited" would work there, explained a supervisor. Other groups or activities indicated other qualities in employees. Often, "the mentally unstable" worked within home-help service groups, a supervisor explained. They were deemed suitable to take care of old people suffering from dementia, who were said to require "a kind of slow-motion environment in order to feel really good." The supervisor thought: "There, I believe Samhall employees have a sureness of aim," especially since he thought that people with their kinds of occupational disabilities could be presumed to find it easier to relate to the situation of the older people. According to the supervisor: "Many older people, and in particular those with dementia, also have a functional disorder when it comes to intellect." Hence, "disabled people are able to help other disabled people," he concluded.

A psychologist hired by Samhall who was in charge of a training course for a group of occupationally disabled employees about "encounters in institutional care" with old people in a home for the elderly where Samhall had an operation believed that "Many elderly people have a disruption in communication, which also applies to Samhall's personnel, and that is why they suit each other so well." One of Samhall's annual reports maintained that work with the elderly was appropriate for the occupationally disabled:

Employees at Samhall work with assignments that are adapted after each individual functional disorder. – Within elder care it is by no means a disadvantage to have a slow work pace, especially when it comes to contacts with the elderly themselves. In this way, work within elder care suits so many of Samhall's employees more than well.

Disability as Competence

As the leading subcontractor to private and public organizations in Sweden, Samhall has to encompass a wide range of occupational disabilities to be able to operate as comprehensive a business enterprise as possible, where specific occupationally disabled employees can be matched to specific jobs. For this reason, "We want to have a variety of jobs in order to be able to achieve adaptation for the individual. People have different handicaps," explained a leading Samhall manager. Persons who have been classified as of low intellect, having minimal talent and being mentally retarded are regarded as suitable for certain tasks, while people with social phobias, addictions or other 'asocial behavior' are considered suitable for other ones. As Samhall's CEO explained: "If we are to successfully tackle assignments, we must have a mixture of different functional disorders and different impairments. We can't only have people with grave disabilities. We are trying to run this like any other company."

This view was reflected in a report in a staff magazine from a unit where it was emphasized that they could offer a "broad selection – to the benefit of both employees and customers." The report stated that the division manager had "fought for a long time to win sympathy for a unit or work area that includes a variety of different work assignments for the employees to choose between," for "How else will we be able to create good possibilities for development, when perhaps around ten or so different disability groups are represented among employees?" In another story, there was a report from one of Samhall's seven units where cabling is installed. The work involves fine stripping of conductors, installing pins and contacts, and marking the cables and subsequently testing them: "This production is suitable for Samhall employees. Here we have both simple and more difficult operational phases" – work for different kinds of disability groups, where different work routines organize the behavior of different occupationally disabled employees. One supervisor explained: "We have learned that some occupationally disabled people are good at certain things, such as installing chassis. All people can't do everything. Some groups have become very adept with certain kinds of fixtures. We can't just move people around, for then we will come up against problems with quality." Similar jobs that workers with low intellect were regarded as being particularly suitable for could be found at several other work places. One supervisor called it "idiotically simple jobs for a normal person," but it "makes them happy, at least they have something to do."

Chapter 7
Developing Teamwork

The Samhall internal Website states: "The purpose of development through work is the development of knowledge, ability and social competence and motivation. The way of organizing work helps not only the learning of the individual but also that of the group." Consequently, working methods "should be open and provide an opportunity for collaboration and the exchange of experiences. Work in production should be organized in work teams in order to provide employees with added responsibility and room for personal actions and decisions." In this connection, a central tenet of Samhall's personnel development is "work should be based on group organization" where the work team is given "a central role in production." It is specified that "the group, which should not be larger than around ten people," which one assumes will prevent any employee ending up as an outsider:

> should as far as possible produce or be responsible for a finished component or even better, a product. Job rotation is a natural element in group-oriented work. It must be possible for work teams to receive and even take added responsibility if they are really going to be able to influence production goals. For example, this can be accomplished by having the group participate in problem solving during production setup and when selecting the means of production.

Occupationally disabled employees at Samhall in most cases work in groups, and much of the practical work on such activities as manufacturing a fire-proof locker in one place, a sanitary cabinet in another or electric fittings at a third work place takes place in a group. This group work is a part of the Developing Work Place (DWP), and this perspective is intended to promote the exchange of experiences among the employees in their capacity as occupationally disabled individuals, creating requirements for collective action where each person is part of a process of mutual development. The appropriateness of this action is based on the organizational expectations that prevail about the occupationally disabled, which are manifested in work routines for them, and which, for example, differ from the work routines for supervisors.

New employees normally learn operations by accompanying a co-worker in the group who demonstrates what is to be done and what different things entail – for example, what is involved in "cleaning the dung from a stable" or "grooming a horse" – as well as how these activities should be carried out. As one employee said: "When a new fellow worker is to be trained in the job, a tutor is assigned who provides support and assistance," as set out in an article in the staff magazine.

The job of the tutor often concerns the execution of the job itself – how to clean staircases, how to fry fish, how to dress for each operation, and so on. A supervisor within a cleaning facility reported:

> The new employees go around together for the first few days. They are allowed to try things themselves, then they are told how to do things and the like, and then they go around with someone else who cleans for the rest of the month. During this period, they are entered into the cleaning training program and then they gain more insights into what they are doing. They understand the training program better, they receive more basic information about "why this and that is cleaned."

After "accompanying," as one supervisor put it, the new employee is usually allowed to try out the job himself or herself under the supervision of co-workers in the group. A new employee in a home-help service group said: "You observe other personnel and try to imitate them, those who have worked a little longer or have training." During one operation, a younger new employee in a industrial facility dealing with wood was working with an older co-worker who helped him to design a frame for a stepladder – where the nails and tacks should be located, how and where the hinges should be attached and so on. The younger worker carefully followed the older worker's movements and work technique, and after the work was completed, the older worker gave the younger worker a number of written templates that he could use as a guide the next time the work was to be carried out.

At another work place, an employee had changed work groups and was about to begin work on welding shelves in sheet steel cabinets. At first, the man accompanied a person who carefully showed him how the welding should be carried out, both with regard to the appearance of the finished result ("neat and tidy without any large marks") as well as how it should feel ("no sharp edges or cavities"). Then the beginner himself was allowed to try, but with regular stoppages for instruction from co-workers in the group.

One supervisor observed that the occupationally disabled employees worked in an "extremely group-oriented" way, and that if there was someone "sitting and carrying on with his own thing, they try to get them into the group." Group work implies that "everyone is included" and "no one is forgotten," another supervisor explained. Work teams often work close to each other, "they take care of each other," one supervisor said, for example by sitting beside each other at a large table sorting such things as nails, condoms, lip balsam, packets of cigarettes or other items in one of Samhall's packaging facilities. During the actual work process at a work place, employees often observe each other, and if anyone deviates from how cigarettes are traditionally packaged, for example, one or more co-workers often comments on this with an "I see, you are doing it in that way." In other cases they say, "You're doing it wrong," and intervene by showing how it 'should' be done instead. For example, one new employee at a unit where one of the operations involved preparing books for re-covering used both his hands when ripping the spine off the book, which deviated from the behavior of others in the group, who instead used their right hand for ripping and their left hand for cutting with a knife. This employee was repeatedly told by a co-worker not to continue ripping with both hands, since "This is the wrong way."

Certainly, in a good many work places there were no "fixed places," as another supervisor pointed out, but those that "know the job often remain." Neither did most employees change groups, but normally worked in the same work group and thus had the same work assignments for longer periods. The same applied between work places: as a rule, people worked at one and the same work place. In other words, the work teams tended to remain unchanged, and there was usually little mobility between work assignments or between the teams. One supervisor felt that on the whole, the occupationally disabled "do not appreciate the idea of job rotation, they feel safe with that they have, of knowing what they have to do in the morning." Another supervisor explained: "Many of our employees have failures behind them which makes them fearful of failing again." Yet another supervisor stressed: "There mustn't be that much variation in the work. It is important that the occupationally disabled can do the same thing for a long time so that they can learn it and feel safe with it." This attitude was not only communicated directly through the supervisors, but also in the staff magazine and videos, where the benefits of working on repetitive assignments in the work teams were often emphasized, despite the principles of the Developing Work Place that stress job rotation between work teams.

In a report in the staff magazine, there was a story about one of the employees who worked on changing covers on video cassettes: "This is a great job. Exactly the kind of job I like most of all. Others may think that it seems monotonous, but that is what suits me. My head spins when there is too much variation, or when I have to tackle several things at the same time." One supervisor thought that the reason his employees invariably worked on the same thing each day for long periods was that "most of them are mentally frail. As soon as something happens outside the framework of things, things don't go well. This is the way our employees function."

The fact that most supervisors did not organize recurrent changes in work was for them an act of safeguarding the development and rehabilitation of the occupationally disabled. It was generally assumed that since the employees were regarded as occupationally disabled individuals, they needed a relatively constant work environment. But there was also a need to guarantee production based on business economic principles. This is stressed as being important in a CD-ROM for supervisors at Samhall:

> By alternating between work assignments, it is possible for a person to develop and learn new things. From the point of view of health, this is generally advantageous. However, for people with functional disorders, it can sometimes be an obstruction. Instead of having to adapt a single operation, perhaps several

operations must be adapted in order for them to work for an occupationally disabled employee, and so on. This investment may be judged as being too great for the unit.

In this context, one of the occupationally disabled employees thought that if new assignments were required within a work group or if it was necessary to change a work group that was not motivated by the need for changes in production at the work place, "you have to be tough yourself and take an initiative. There isn't any supervisor who will come and give you new assignments." One of her colleagues observed: "You are located at a site, and then you remain there." Another employee said: "Many supervisors think that we cannot tackle new things. If we never try anything new, but just sit doing the same job all the time, well, in the end you just don't dare." A supervisor explained that she "never forces the occupationally disabled to do anything. It's better if they come to me themselves and say that they want to do something else." A colleague of hers was of the opinion that "I can't motivate them to change. It must come from them themselves." A government study maintained that personal development of Samhall's occupationally disabled employees:

> should be based on the needs of the employees, the customers and the activities. From the point of view of the employees, the purpose of the development process is professional and personal development. Samhall's leaders should support the employee in the development process, while also emphasizing the employee's personal responsibility for his or her development. The primary factor for success is the employee's resources and commitment.

Thus, the responsibility for change in the content of work lies ultimately with the occupationally disabled employee.

One occupationally disabled employee thought: "Many supervisors are so kind. You don't have to change if you don't want to. After a time, you get scared of changing." Another employee said: "It's up to you if you want to sit there all your life packaging nails, no one will encourage you to move. If you don't take an initiative, you will stay there." Another person was of the opinion that "You have to take a personal initiative if you want development," but "It is difficult. People don't want to make any changes in the groups." A colleague of his argued: "Some people monopolize the more advanced assignments, and we others can't get to them. The boss says that we have to resolve this within the group." An employee who was group leader at a packaging factory observed: "People don't let go of their packaging tables. They don't dare change. They are afraid." In this connection, a man working in a large-scale kitchen said: "It's strange that my fellow workers don't want to learn new things. They flinch at every new thing." In his opinion, there were enough time and resources to learn new work assignments, for example by people exchanging jobs within or between work teams, but "people remain where they are and prefer to do the same thing all the time." He thought:

"The bosses are not committed. They tell us to change, but then nothing happens. People work with their own thing."

Usually, supervisors had a better overview of what assignments were available at the work place in question or other ones than the occupationally disabled employees did, thanks to their contacts with colleagues there. One of the occupationally disabled employees said, "My boss says that there are many other jobs than this one, but doesn't show them to me," and thought, "She should give me an opportunity to change jobs." Her supervisor felt, "They shouldn't have to think about personal development. That is my responsibility. Many of them don't know what's best for them," and pointed out: "Usually the occupationally disabled need a stable existence. Many have previously felt troubled, and that is why they have come here."

Chapter 8
Structuring Behavior

Employees at Samhall come from a wide range of backgrounds: the level of education can vary greatly within the same work place, as well as previous working life experience. In one factory with around seventy employees, there were almost twenty nationalities, several highly educated people (but with different specializations, such as graduate engineer, graduate economist and dentist), ex-miners, carpenters, seamstresses, cleaners, truck drivers and so on. In addition, there were people with different physiological limitations, such as motor disabilities, brain damage, and visual and hearing impairments. However, by organizing the practical work on the basis of more or less distinct work routines, homogeneity in the development of the occupationally disabled can be achieved, which also has the secondary advantage of making the production of electric fittings, sanitary cabinets or cleaning of stairwells efficient. An employee at a Samhall restaurant explained that "there are no conflicts at all at work," despite the fact that the unit included people from different parts of the former Yugoslavia who had come to Sweden as a result of the war between the ethnic groups to which they belonged. An employee wrote in a book about Samhall (Aulin, 2001), under the heading "Fantastic that it Works!", that it was "amazing" that Samhall functioned despite the wide range of disabilities that were said to exist in the units.

One supervisor emphasized the value of the routine character of the work in coping with personal and social problems:

> If you take those that are not mentally retarded but perhaps have a criminal background or an asocial behavior, they often come here to learn how to be punctual, learn how to get on in a group, learn how to deal with one's feelings. Sometimes they can have a fit of rage so they have to learn how to handle all of these things.

Another supervisor described one of his employees who was "world champion at screwing things up" when he started at Samhall and spread "chaos around him. There was no order at all." After many long discussions – "nag, nag, nag" – and first and foremost by working in a storeroom where the demands for a system and order prevailed, his behavior changed: "Now there is fantastic order. He was 'converted,'" the supervisor declared.

A document about Samhall's personnel development concepts observes:

> Unlike many of the environments which people frequent during the hours of the day, the work place has a strict *structure*. People are punctual. There are

certain repetitive elements such as mealtimes and breaks that are introduced in a systematic fashion. Work assignments are well defined and possible to solve.

This is said to be worthwhile, especially for the occupationally disabled, who are often assumed to have experienced some form of personal crisis or depression:

> Because they are tired and distressed and feeble, they do not deal with their environment. In certain mental states, *disunion* is a disabling symptom. The person cannot remain in an activity, but throws himself or herself between different jobs and divides his or her attention between lots of different things. A well-structured environment like a work place can contribute towards making a person with mental and social problems feel so much better that a positive process is initiated.

Structured Work and its Consequences

Since most of the work is structured, one of the occupationally disabled employees experienced that she had even "brought order to her private life" thanks to her employment. She explained that her job at Samhall involved weighing raw materials for food production, which required "precision and a feeling for numbers." She reported: "I have become much more precise at home after working on this." In this context, a government study about vocational rehabilitation listed a number of "indicators" in people who required rehabilitation through participation in a structured working life, such as "lack of focus; insufficient ability to prioritize; lack of vision or future prospects; insufficient project and action planning; insufficient participation," which were all factors that implied organization through work.

A leading official at Samhall was of the opinion that "People look for some kind of structure. The child looks for structure. The teenager looks for structure. Adults look for structure and frameworks. The elderly look for structure. We need some form of controllable reality in order to successively tackle change." Several supervisors encouraged the occupationally disabled to carry out their work in compliance with the routine, and criticized them if they felt that the order created by the routines has been disrupted. For example, during a visit to a refrigeration room where one of the employees worked on sorting perishables, one supervisor thought, "It is messy here," and pointed out that "There should be order here similar to that in a library." Some work places deploy so-called quality systems that are organized around formal work routines: "We have a well-developed quality system and a large classification system worked out here," as one supervisor explained, entailing that the different operations should be carried out in a certain way, which was supported by photos and written documents specifying correct execution. Deviations from the work routine should be reported so that they can be followed up using so-called corrective measures, where "the personnel learn how things should be carried out so that they do not repeat errors," one supervisor explained.

Another supervisor in an IT unit where they worked on tasks such as electronic filing said: "It is important that work is carried out in a uniform way. People should work in the same way. They should not deviate from the job description."

Even if the work content at Samhall work places usually changes – for example, one day an employee at a restaurant may be packaging hundreds of portions of pancakes and thick pea soup, and the next day hundreds of portions of fish with mashed potatoes, or at a site where books are "converted," one week the employee may be ripping up fictional works, then factual study books the following week, or at one packaging facility, one month condoms may be packaged, while next month it may be lip balsam – the actual character of the work remains unchanged: repetition. One of Samhall's cleaners expressed it as: "Each day is like any other. I know this job by heart." Another employee distributing food by car each morning according to a fixed driving schedule observed as he put the key in the ignition: "I can do this job in my sleep." Or as a third employee explained: "I don't think about what I'm doing. It all goes automatically." One occupationally disabled employee who worked on soldering components declared: "Soldering is soldering. It's the same thing all the time regardless of what you are soldering." A supervisor at a warehouse for lamps explained: "The object of the job is to pick, pack and sort, but naturally, it doesn't matter if the products are motor car bulbs or ordinary electric lightbulbs."

Neither does the repetitive element in the job differ between groups or between work units. Soldering components, packaging frozen food, preparing journals for microfilming or scanning, or cleaning stairwells imply no great variations in the collective supply of work at Samhall. A unit head at a packaging industry explained: "People learn things when they repeat the same thing over and over again." One supervisor agreed, saying: "Each product has its own routines, but in some way they are quite similar."

Supervisors encouraged their employees to work in a repetitive way. One supervisor who circulated between tables in a packaging industry where different work teams sorted and packaged thousands of packets of cigarettes for a few weeks, told his personnel, "You are so clever," and "This is going well." Another supervisor told a newly employed occupationally disabled worker on his first day at work in a warehouse: "There are a lot of routines here. Learn them. Don't stress. Don't do anything different." A manager at an external work place where Samhall personnel sorted collected clothing and where the work amounted to taking clothes from unsorted sacks and placing them into four different boxes, said: "It's uncanny how clever disabled people are at this." A unit head at a mechanical workshop where the personnel worked in different teams with specific tasks thought: "Many of them are really good if you give them a framework to work within. Yes, many of them are very able. They work on the basis of their ability." Another supervisor who explained that the unit "offered simple packaging work" often returned to the fact that the personnel were "really good" at their work, which, for example, could involve packaging thousands of electric lightbulbs for a month. In this context, a colleague of his thought: "It is important that attention is drawn to the positive behavior of the occupationally disabled." Several supervisors stressed that many of the employees were unable to successfully tackle tasks that were too extensive by referring to the fact that they were occupationally disabled. One supervisor said that it was "important to break down the job into small portions." A colleague of his declared: "It's about organizing the job so that it's easy to learn."

Neither do new orders and commissions for jobs present any significant variation in the basic repetition. The fact that the design of electric fittings manufactured at a unit is changed does not mean that the work for the occupationally disabled is changed beyond perhaps the addition of one component and the disappearance of another. One supervisor declared that the work: "implies repetition. It is the pattern they recognize. There is different content in the repetition."

In this context, the fact that people with different personal backgrounds basically perform the same work assignments is of less significance: "It doesn't really matter what type of job it is, disabled people function in the same way," a supervisor explained. Regardless of whether you are a highly educated academic who has previously worked on administrative assignments, or you are a former miner, or you have never had a professional job before, or if you come from another country, Samhall offers a similar working environment founded on the concept of an adapted working environment for the occupationally disabled based on the execution of certain work routines. One supervisor explained: "The work suits most of them. We have standardized and simplified most processes." One of the employees commented on this, "We are different. We function differently, but we are not treated differently," and another employee who worked at portioning out meals on an assembly line said: "Even if I were a director of economy, I could end up here."

One of Samhall's former press relations officers who wrote a book in 1990 about her time at Samhall, described her impressions after a visit to a work place:

> The occupationally disabled sit each at his or her own work table, which in turn makes up parts of a large common work table. On the common work table, there is a large carton with nails. The occupationally disabled employees pick nails from the box and place these nails in smaller packages. I assume that I have been unlucky and contact the regional CEO immediately. Surely, this is not meaningful work. Inside me, I just want him to tell me that it is a mistake. However, he smiles at me in a friendly manner. These are only temporary work assignments while waiting for other assignments to come in. Back at the corporate head office, I tell people about my visit during a mutual coffee break with a few fellow colleagues with many years at Samhall. I'm still waiting for a reassuring answer. However, one of the branch-hardened employees answers, "Well, if you've seen one workshop, you've seen them all." The others nod in agreement (Rådahl 1990: 20).

In the same book, the author tells of a woman at a work place who:

takes a bundle of white yarn from a large, brown cardboard box, places the bundle in the sewing machine and sews a straight seam through it. She changes the position of the sewing machine and reverses – sews a straight seam. She sews two seams through the bundle of yarn: one forward and one back. The floor mop is finished. She takes a new bundle of yarn. Sews one straight seam forward and one straight seam backwards. She takes a new bundle of yarn. "Is this her work – the thing she does for eight hours a day?", I carefully wonder. Hulda Malmbo [the employee] smiles and says that this is what she mainly does. However, sometimes when it feels a little too monotonous, she exchanges work assignments with the woman who cuts the yarn into long threads. ... But for the most part, she sews floor mops (Rådahl 1990: 36).

Underemployment

Many Samhall units are characterized by "underemployment," as it is referred to internally – there is not enough work, or no work at all. The result of this is that many of the daily work routines are eliminated. Several thousands of employees have been affected by this for many years. A recent government study declared:

> A fundamental starting point is that Samhall should offer work. It is in the nature of things that within a company like Samhall with its special assignments, there has always existed a certain amount of underemployment in the context that employees with occupational disabilities have had limited assignments or have completely lacked mission. Earlier, this underemployment has been relatively limited and even worked as an incentive in finding new business sectors and subsequently new work activities for employees with occupational disabilities. In the light of a receding demand and the fact that employees with occupational disabilities are not laid off due to shortage of work, there is significant underemployment.

In a report in a magazine from 2003 titled "Those that are always left over," there was a story about the personnel at one of Samhall's packaging workshops who did not have anything to work with, as "many types of industrial jobs that previously were available within Samhall have been moved to 'low-price countries.'" At many units, the personnel might come in the morning, and after clocking in have no work-related activities to carry out. One employee wrote in a book about Samhall:

> We just sit around and have nothing to do, and then we sit in a room where there are no fans. When it rains, the rain drops through the roof and onto us. All managers and supervisor are surly. They don't say anything about how things will go. We have sat like this, no work since last Christmas. Should it be like this in a state-owned company? (Aulin, 2001).

One supervisor declared that underemployment often created "disarray," and explained: "The occupationally disabled become completely confused." Another supervisor pointed out: "They don't know what to do. They sit around crying and the like. If there is no work, then there is nothing to grasp hold of." A supervisor at an external work place where Samhall had personnel witnessed that Samhall's personnel "function very well" for the most part, except when there is little to do, "Then they are forced to look for work and don't know where to fix their attention. Should they clean the floor, pick up old paper or what? Many of them feel stressed about this. A lot of work is better, then people know what to do." An occupationally disabled employee agreed: "It's difficult not having work, for then one doesn't know what to do." Another supervisor explained: "Things become very anxious here, as we have little to do." In that respect, the lack of work at several units had given rise to anxiety, another supervisor thought: "Here, many lack work. They become like the guys in the *Muppet Show*. They run about anxiously or they just sit staring." One of the employees said that among her co-workers at another work place where there was no work, "They just sit twiddling their thumbs until they become dizzy in the head." In an interview in a magazine, one of the occupationally disabled employees said: "There is a lot of trouble and a lot of drivel when there isn't a lot to do." At one unit where there was no work to do, the occupationally disabled workers wandered to and fro in the factory premises until a supervisor told them to "go and sit down" at their work tables, where they clasped their hands and sat silently.

The magazine report referred to above stated: "With the decrease in demand for industrial jobs, there is very little to do here. Sometimes days of now work at all. The employees sit around the large tables just waiting for something to do. No activity other than sitting on one's chair and gazing." One of the employees interviewed declared: "The whole of last year we had hardly anything to do, and it seem as if the bosses don't want us running round that much. The best thing is if we just sit here, staring." At another work place, several people sat reading newspapers, some slept, and others listened to the radio. At a third work site, people sat in groups chatting with each other. In an internal video, one woman related: "There is nothing to do" and "We take coffee breaks and read newspapers." A colleague of hers said, "It's no fun," and added that she came from a unit where they had not had anything to do for six months, and that it was not much different at the unit where he was working now, even if here there were "at least a few jobs."

To this formally routine-free existence, many of the occupationally disabled reacted in a similar, routine way. Despite the obvious freedom in terms of schedule, they took coffee breaks at the stipulated times, had lunch during the normal lunchbreak, and went home when the formal working day was over. A common type of behavior was sitting at their work places and just staring out into the room or reading a newspaper. At some work places, the supervisors took action by "giving them a few therapy assignments" in the form of "reading English, taking walks or the like," one supervisor reported. As well as initiatives among supervisors, there were also general company efforts. In an eight-page document on the Samhall internal Website, "What to Do when Not Fully Booked," 85 suggestions of suitable activities for the occupationally disabled personnel are provided. As in the case of work-specific activities at Samhall, the various suggestions for activities involve creating organized work activity, which is a core value for Samhall. The formal working hours, that employees arrive at specific times, that coffee breaks are taken at specific times, that lunch is eaten during half an hour in the middle of the day and that there is a coffee break in the afternoon, constitute the basic organization of the working day. Thus, it is less important what is being done by the occupationally disabled at the individual work place, and more important that *something* is being done in an organized way, including particular activities related to underemployment, such as sitting quietly around a table. As Samhall's Director of Communications wrote in the staff magazine under the heading, "We Must Not Lose Sight of Our Message": "It isn't what we do, but who does it that is the unique thing with Samhall."

Routinizing Private Life

In a similar way that anxiety and problems could arise due to the lack of work routines during the working day itself, a number of supervisors were of the opinion that leisure time for many of the occupationally disabled employees created problems for them due to the lack of routine: "For many of them, long periods of free time such as at Christmas and the summer vacations are a worry, since they have nothing to do," one supervisor explained. For this reason, Samhall sometimes offers organized excursions. "There are really great supervisors who use their free time and arrange excursions during holidays," a nurse in Samhall's corporate health service explained. However, more comprehensive in character are the "keep-fit activities" that Samhall organizes, which are presented as part of the company's personnel development activities for the occupationally disabled.

An article in Samhall's staff magazine stated, "Life is full of conflicts, demands and strains of different kinds," which leads to the question, "What is it that allows certain people to successfully tackle difficult experiences and situations and still keep their health?" The answer that was forthcoming was "intelligibility – the feeling of having order, structure and clarity in everyday life and life, manageability – the feeling of being able to encounter difficulties and get through them and the feeling of meaningfulness in life." It went on to say, "We all have a personal responsibility [for our health], for example through our lifestyle and living habits, but there is also an employer and social responsibility for developing and creating good soil for health and well-being." A report in the staff magazine, "Active Fun!", included a statement that "Keep-fit activities are an important part of Samhall's personnel development," and these are coordinated by Samhall's corporate health service. A supervisor who was interviewed thought: "For me, keep-fit activities are the same as having fun together. Therefore, I really want to encourage my personnel to begin such activities."

For similar reasons, Samhall also offers organized "vacation courses" – courses for both the occupationally disabled employees and their families. The purpose of these is to offer "a stimulating and meaningful vacation for the occupationally disabled," one of the course arrangers declared. For instance, in the course program for 2004 on the theme "participation and development," the occupationally disabled employees were given the opportunity of "meeting other employees from other Samhall companies with whom you can exchange experiences." In an article in the staff magazine, one participant said: "It was exciting to meet Samhall employees from other places, with different disabilities and backgrounds." In another report in the magazine, there was a description that "Samhall's courses are for our employees who want an active vacation filled with experiences, good food, socializing and a good laugh." The report went on to say that various "competitions and games" for the occupationally disabled were interspersed with lectures, for example from a bank "providing advice and tips on how to make your money go further." One person who had attended each summer for fifteen years was interviewed: "Many people taking part are quite lonely," he explained. As a rule, Samhall's CEO used to participate for a day or two, and observed: "What a fantastic opportunity for a vacation."

In addition to the keep-fit activities offered during working hours, the purpose of which is to organize the behavior of the employees during breaks from work or outside work hours, as well as creating an opportunity for socializing between the occupationally disabled employees, the staff magazine also provides advice from time to time about suitable behavior during the work day and about an appropriate way of living even during leisure time. In an article on the theme "love and social life," dealing with "love at work," a couple described how they met at one of Samhall's work places, which is not unusual, according to one supervisor. The article explained how the couple met, that they just "clicked," and that "I felt that he liked me," one of them declared. The article went on to say, "They are now planning their future," and related how their mutual boss gave them guidance on how to behave in an appropriate way at the work place. In fact, the supervisor had "to put a halt to Elisabeth's and Per-Olof's tokens of affection during working hours" – for example, they were not allowed "to kiss and cuddle during working hours."

In another report in the staff magazine, under the heading "Hands On the Comforter!", the relationship of the mentally retarded toward sex was discussed – "Being different can imply an increased risk, both of being treated badly and of treating others badly" – as well as the fact that many occupationally disabled people "do not understand what happens in the body and emotional life." Thus, it is important to "learn where the limits are set." In conclusion, the question was asked, "Perhaps Samhall's supervisors should be trained in questions dealing with the sexuality of the mentally retarded?", and information was provided about a homepage on the Internet that could provide information about "sexuality and functional disorders."

Samhall does not merely reach out to employees in their free time, but also when they are on the sick list for a long period. An article in the staff magazine describes supervisors and work groups taking responsibility "for maintaining contact with fellow employees that are on the sick list for a long time," and in an internal video there is a description of how one of the employees who was on the sick list visited her work place each day to socialize with her co-workers. She explained how she had "been given permission to go there for a while and drink coffee and meet friends. I'm happy about that, for I need it for the sake of my social life." Thus, Samhall offers an organized environment for its occupationally disabled employees by practicing different routines, not only at work, but also during leisure time. To that extent, "Samhall is more than a job," as one of its latest slogans states.

Chapter 9
Specializing Behavior

Employment as an occupationally disabled person at Samhall basically involves specialization of competencies through the division of labor. At the large-scale kitchen described earlier, food production began with a work group in the goods department receiving the raw materials from a supplier, checking these, then placing them in specific locations on the premises, such as cold storage rooms, refrigerators or dry storage areas. These raw materials were then used by the work group, which "processed" the food, preparing it for cooking by cutting open bags of peeled potatoes, ready-cut onions, already parboiled broccoli and so on.

Then the group which actually carried out the cooking of the food took over, where one person fried, another person boiled potatoes, and a third prepared the gravy. All finished food was transported on trays to a group that placed portions in plastic packages that were subsequently marked with the contents, cooled down, then placed in a cold storage room for distribution to customers.

The same division of tasks was evident in a workshop where such goods as fire-proof lockers were manufactured. The manufacturing itself involved a number of operations carried out by a number of groups where different people had different assignments, but where each assignment was a part of a larger manufacturing chain, such as stores management, machining, cutting to size, pressing and bending of sheet metal, joining and spot welding, varnishing, and final assembly and packaging.

Closely related assignments within a unit can also be found within work groups where the individual members work on a specific assignment, but where each assignment is a part of a larger production process. For example, in a packaging unit, a team worked on packing windshield wipers. One person picked up the windscreen wipers and their various parts and distributed them among a number of employees who assembled them, which entailed installing a small spigot on a rail that secured the rubber blade to the rail itself. The packages themselves were supplied to the workshop as flat packs, so another employee folded these, placed the wipers in them, then handed them over to a person who attached labels indicating the type of wiper blade. A third employee glued the packages together and placed them in piles, which another worker stacked ready for distribution to customers.

Overall, the linking of the separate assignments of each disabled employee, group, department or unit constituted a "combined operation," where employees assembled parts in the practical phase and combined these into a whole based on a division of labor where each individual concentrated on a limited assignment. This combined operation could be carried by the same person, who had a number of articles on a table in front of him or her (such as the parts for a windshield wiper that was to be assembled, or parts of an electric fitting that were to be assembled in a certain way to create a specific product). Alternatively, different people could carry out the assembly in a manufacturing chain (for example, different work groups manufactured different parts of a stepladder or different parts of a sanitary cabinet). In these cases, the product only took shape or manifested itself in the final link of the work chain.

In that respect, the work can be likened to fitting the pieces together to form a completed job, where all activities in a large-scale kitchen, for example, are controlled by the menus and recipes put together by the supervisor. The raw materials for the food consisted of partly prepared products, such as ready-cut onions, peeled potatoes or ready-rolled meatballs, that were refined through frying, boiling and so on and subsequently packed in single-portion packages. Electric fittings were assembled at a factory according to drawings from a customer which showed how the various components should be assembled. The assembly followed specific work routines, in part according to the components that were used, and in part according to the specified procedures that existed for assembly of the parts – how cables should be connected and run, where different parts should be mounted and so forth.

Therefore, it is of central importance that each employee learns to carry out certain specific work routines associated within his or her role in the work chain. For example, a newly employed disabled person at an industrial facility received instructions from a co-worker about how he should assemble different controls and how the cables should be connected. The acquisition of these routines entailed criticizing him when he deviated from the routine, followed by praise when he complied with it. The learning itself was based on the fact that the person in question observed his co-worker and adapted himself to her comments regarding the various operations that were to be performed. In this respect, there was a need to teach standardized operations and use of working materials, which demanded that the beginner followed the same procedure as the instructor, since if he deviated from this, the instructor would not be able to show how the rest of the assembly should be carried out.

Sometimes the occupationally disabled employees did not have any knowledge of why they did certain things at all, or of how the assignments they carried out were linked to other activities in a manufacturing chain. One person working on assembling electric fittings brushed heavy oil on one nut for each part of a fixture that she had put together, which was essential for the next stage in the assembly. She did not know why she was applying this heavy oil, but this knowledge was not necessary for the job she was carrying out. She worked with a limited set of assignments in a work team, carried them out in accordance with a work routine, then passed on her partly assembled electric fittings in an organized chain of labor division. This division of labor within the different Samhall units (which, in certain cases, was even manifested by a physical separation between work groups) is made possible by carrying out certain routines that are linked to each other, implying that the same person does not need to carry out all phases. There is a linking of routines, and consequently of behavior, in a larger manufacturing chain, where each person's individual behavior is part of a larger organized whole.

Thus, within each work group and department there was a limited and specified number of assignments – feeding planks into a machine or standing on the other side and receiving them, cleaning stairs or offices, preparing food by placing onions and ground meat in roasting pans or frying food, ironing or mangling and so on. One supervisor gave an example of a situation in an unit manufacturing electric fittings, where the stores had previously been "spread out, a little here and a little there" and where the employees had to go and assemble the work materials in the form of collector rails, wiring, screws, nuts and so forth that were needed for the actual assembly of the electric fittings: "Naturally, things were completely chaotic and there was no order," he said, explaining how eventually they built a storeroom in a separate part of the building where only designated personnel were allowed. The people who worked there had no previous experience of working in a storeroom, but "eventually became really good at it by carrying out their operation repetitively." One of the occupationally disabled employees also felt this was a positive thing: "Each person here does his job. It's nice not having to think about what the others are doing."

Much of the specialization that employment at Samhall implies not only comes from interpersonal contact between the occupationally disabled employees themselves, but also from the way they interact with a variety of tools and materials. At many work places, employees have tools at their disposal which are often specific to certain work groups. In a workshop where electric fittings were manufactured, each work place had a set of ordinary screwdrivers, hammers, pliers and so on, as well as miscellaneous special tools. In a large-scale kitchen, there was a lot of work equipment in the form of cookers, ovens, washing machines and cold storage facilities, in addition to utensils such as ladles, measures and spatulas. These and other tools/utensils both enable and prevent certain activities by the occupationally disabled employees. Some tools can only be used for a special electric fitting and are also only suitable for specific manufacturing procedures. For example, some cartons in a storeroom can only be assembled in a certain way, in accordance with the established packing rules; certain loading pallets can only be lifted in a specific way using a special machine; some cables can only be mounted in certain contacts on a collector rail for lighting fittings in a specific way, in accordance with the prevailing division of labor.

Sometimes the occupationally disabled employees were supplied with so-called "standard models" – completed models of products to be manufactured which had been made by the supervisors, such as a finished stepladder, a completed electric fitting or a finished changing locker. A person working on running wires for a large electric fitting took a standard model of this product and examined it to see how the cables should be routed. The same applied in a workshop where people were soldering components for medical equipment. Initially, the personnel sat next to a standard model and imitated the model until they no longer needed to look at it.

Workers placed welds in the same places as on the standard model and attached components and cables in the same way, thus gradually developing competence.

Work instructions constituted an additional source for the specialization of competencies. These were written either directly by the customer – for example, how lightbulbs or batteries were to be packaged – or by a supervisor based on customer orders, as was the case with the menus that one supervisor in a large-scale kitchen composed each week based on the customer's order for a certain amount of homely fare. According to the supervisor, this "kitchen planning" enabled "the employees to know what to do," and it was evident who would do what and how it should be done. At one work place, the supervisor specified "driving lists" for the distribution of food carried out for the home-care service, "so that they don't waste time driving around." The driving lists not only specified the routes the personnel should follow to the housing areas in question, they also described how they should pack the cars they were using to accommodate the driving schedule.

Certainly, in some instances the work instructions were also less detailed, which was often the case for the shopping lists that Samhall personnel used when purchasing perishables for retired citizens, where, for example, only "orange marmalade" might be written. One of the employees commented: "Sometimes, the customers do not clearly specify what they want, and then errors can result. Then we may have to go back and return the goods." Thus, it was always important to keep to the instructions supplied by the customer, and not to try to improvise. In the work carried out at one site in the morning, where foodstuffs were packaged for the home-care service for further distribution to retired citizens, packing lists were mounted on the walls and these were carefully followed. Plastic bags, on which fellow workers had written the name of customer, were filled with whatever the customer had specified – such as milk or a box containing warm food.

Not infrequently, a photo of the different stages of work and the final result was attached to the instructions, showing what a motor-car lamp case should look like, for instance. As a rule, the supervisors took photographs of the completed results and attached these to the different stages of work in the job descriptions. Employees then had to study the photos and job instructions and try to carry out the work in accordance with them, rather than personally experimenting with the material. For example, at one workshop the different stages of work that were deemed important for distributing incoming goods to the stores were illustrated by photos. There were instructions about how goods should be received, how they should be registered and sorted, as well as where they should be placed in the stores. Often, so-called material cards that accompanied a product through the production chain specifying the different processing stages to be carried out were used in production – for example, the bending of sheet metal and turning and distribution of assignments between employees.

One supervisor at a packaging unit declared:

> We have fairly brief written instructions, or they can be a little longer and
> complemented with photos, which involves making an initial piece. Persons who

can subsequently read this instruction and material content make an initial piece. These persons are present as long as the job lasts and can be consulted by other persons who cannot read or feel that they are not doing things correctly. Say you have a group of six people sitting and working with a motor-car lamp case and you come in, work an afternoon, arrive at around 11.30 a.m. and someone in charge of the table says, "You can take Pelle's place." Well, what has Pelle done? You can then either get help from those sitting next to you or from the person in charge of the table, or you can say, "Can I look at the first piece? What do I have to do?", depending somewhat on what you know. "Where is the instruction? What does it look like, or what can you show me?", so that the opportunity you have in a group depends on where you are yourself: "Can I read? Can I see? Can I listen? Can I get someone to show me?"

At another work place, this philosophy was called "phase work", from which the company "earns a lot of money," a supervisor declared. This entails that "each person does a little bit of a complete job," which some person or persons eventually assemble. The supervisor declared that subsequently, "unskilled workers can work in the work team, since we can initially provide them with simpler jobs."

An additional source for the specialization of behavior based on interaction with items close to the occupationally disabled workers were the machines that many used. Usually, the workshops producing such things as furniture and cabinets had an extensive collection of machinery, which was also the case at several IT units where people worked on filming or scanning filing materials. Above all, many employees had a machine as their "co-worker" with which they worked all day, the machine performing certain elements of the work and the employee others.

At a mechanical workshop, one employee worked with a machine that bent approximately 800 pieces of sheet metal each day. During the course of the work, the machine gave instructions on a display that the worker had to follow in order to carry out the job: "Push in the sheet metal," "Turn the sheet metal," "Turn the plate 180°," and so on. The person acted in accordance with the instructions and confirmed the different activities by depressing a pedal, which in turn resulted in the machine carrying out specific activities and giving new instructions. This machine was pre-programmed by one of the supervisors to perform specific activities adapted to the material and the work to be carried out, in this case fabricating doors for fire-proof lockers.

Many of the jobs at Samhall's heavy industrial workshops involved repetitive interaction with machines, where in general there was little possibility that the employee could affect this interaction. As a rule, the occupationally disabled employees themselves did not program the machines with which they subsequently worked, and did not set a specific fixture in the mechanical machines. Instead, these phases were carried out by the supervisors.

The specialization was also organized using symbols. One supervisor believed that a commonly defined job of cleaning the floor of a factory could be interpreted in far too many ways, and "Since many of my employees have problems with their power of judgment, you can't just tell them, 'This floor has to be cleaned,' for then things will just be chaotic." Instead, she thought that each new cleaning job should be broken down "into bits that they can understand." As an example, she mentioned a job "for mongoloids," which she carefully specified and explained for everybody: "I made it clear for them what they had to do" by drawing different models for the parts of the job – mopping, cleaning with a broom, clearing up gravel with a shovel and vacuuming certain floors. "It is about translating the job to their level and distributing it so that they can manage it," she thought, concluding: "They eventually become experts in a narrow field."

This line of argument was further developed in another example with maps that were mounted on the wall in the personnel room showing the different housing areas to be cleaned. Each map constituted a description of the housing area, and the street door entrances were marked in different colors. The supervisor explained that it was not enough to just mark where cleaning was to be carried out. She believed that one also had to put a cross through those street numbers that should not be cleaned: "Take number 44, for example. There is a daycare center there, but we are not cleaning there. So I have crossed out that number with white-out on the map, otherwise they would go in there and start cleaning." She concluded:

> One has to alter the map of reality so that it is comprehensible to them. There must be clear signs of what has to be done, otherwise things will go wrong immediately. By dividing labor, we teach them to learn what they should and should not do as occupationally disabled employees.

Chapter 10
Motivating Managers

Typically, supervisors at Samhall perceive their work as unique compared to other companies, especially since they find that the employees are different and require specialized treatment: "The job of supervisor at Samhall entails responsibility for the social development of the occupationally disabled. This 'curative' role entails that the job of supervisor at Samhall is decidedly different from supervisory jobs at other work places," as one government study observed.

One supervisor pointed out that as a supervisor, "You can't be too quick or too tough." One of her fellow supervisors who had long experience of working in private industry believed: "Samhall is vastly different compared to other companies, you don't think along the same lines. There is a different mentality. Samhall accepts that it's okay to make a loss. 'We have people with problems,' they say." An "important difference to other companies," one supervisor thought, is that at Samhall you have to have "a lot of patience with people. Our personnel do not work like most people." He exemplified this by explaining that sometimes there could be "serious conflicts and quarrels within the work groups," and "at such times it is important to be calm and try to direct the discussion."

The CEO of Samhall explained:

> I usually say like this at employment interviews, "If you haven't bought in to Samhall's business concept, you shouldn't start work here, for you will never be happy. You will always be confronted with situations where rational decisions are not possible. You must have the idea that Samhall is different." I have seen a lot of people who have come to us who have been really successful outside Samhall but have been terribly frustrated when rational decisions have not been possible. You have to employ other dimensions when making decisions.

One supervisor thought that it was "the human dimension" that drove him in his work:

> You get so much in return. I'm the kind of person who protects people. If the occupationally disabled are ill, I send them a card. I send them Christmas cards, listen to how they feel, and we should do this when they are ill. We show that we are thinking of them, that they haven't been forgotten.

Often, this care for the employees transcended the limitations of the work place and working hours: "My supervisor has visited me at home and met my friends here. I think this is nice," one of the employees recounted in an interview in the staff magazine. Several supervisors in an industrial facility described how they had sometimes gone into town looking for personnel that had not turned up for work, but who had instead "been sitting drinking on a bench," as one supervisor put it, and others had helped employees to arrange accommodation and make contact with the social welfare authorities, the police and the regional Social Insurance Office.

In a report in the staff magazine, there was a story about one of the employees who, with gratitude, explained that his supervisor, "noticed that I was terribly tired at work and wasn't feeling all that well for a time. On that occasion, my supervisor helped me. She arranged for me to work fewer hours. Now I feel better and the job is fun again." In the same spirit, a loving couple at a unit related with gratitude: "Some of our fellow workers said stupid things about us, we felt victimized. But my supervisor, Margit, helped us. She told them to stop." These more personal dimensions of relations with employees make "many supervisors feel that they are carrying out very important and significant work. One motivating factor is the sympathy supervisors say that they feel for the occupationally disabled," a government study reported. The study went on to say: "A driving force [for supervisors] is that they experience that it is very rewarding working with the occupationally disabled on a personal and emotional level." One supervisor pointed out that his job was of particular importance since, "Managers in other companies tell me that 'We don't have the energy to serve as daddies for the disabled.'"

To be a successful supervisor within Samhall requires "a strong psyche. There are problems in all work places, but here there are personal problems all the time, for example with economics. Many of the employees have the bailiffs after them due to addiction problems," observed one supervisor. One Samhall publication maintained that "being a department head and manager at Samhall is a challenge out of the ordinary" by emphasizing the special needs that the occupationally disabled employees have (which is one of the reasons that the training courses in leadership and organization that the supervisors have to take primarily deal with the behavior of the occupationally disabled and how someone who is not occupationally disabled treats the occupationally disabled). Consequently, supervisors saw it as their duty to be present in the daily work for "personnel development reasons," one of them explained. A part of the job is to "make sure that the personnel feel okay," as one supervisor in a mechanical workshop put it. Several of them previously worked at companies other than Samhall: "Compared to being a supervisor out there [in other companies], here we have to be more of a support person. I have to be something of a father, a mother, a psychologist, a man Friday," one of them stressed. Another supervisor expressed the following in a government study:

> Before I came here, I was a supervisor in a mechanical industrial facility. There my work was to check on which order was to be dealt with and then organize and distribute work assignments for the day. My work here is more comprehensive.

Apart from supervisory assignments, I am father, priest and counselor for those working in my team.

More often than not, this is manifested in physical contact in the form of hugs and sometimes kisses: "You can imagine the feeling when you come to work in the morning and get hugged by your fellow [occupationally disabled] workers," another supervisor explained in the same study. In that respect, one supervisor felt that it was important for the occupationally disabled to "be seen and confirmed," and gave the example of a woman "whose day is ruined if she doesn't get a hug in the morning."

The Ideal Samhall Manager

The "ideal supervisor at Samhall" is a person who not only has a "humanistic basic outlook," but also "a businesslike way of thinking," as one member of corporate management put it. Or as the CEO of Samhall stressed: "You can be both rational and a humanist. You don't have to be either the one or the other." However, an official at the NEO who was interviewed in a government study thought that it was difficult to combine these roles: "On the one hand they [the supervisors] should develop personnel, on the other hand they have economic demands made of them," and "these things are not compatible," which was even maintained in a government study that declared: "The supervisors have a difficult role within Samhall. They have to try to maintain efficient production while concurrently also having responsibility for the development of the occupationally disabled."

An official at the NEO was of the opinion that when Samhall recruited supervisors, "it took people from industry who were imbibed with this concept of production, but they didn't know that much about how to develop people." A member of Samhall's corporate management said: "Very many of our supervisors in the industry are much more fixated on the lathe work than on the people behind the lathes – and they can't really help this, because they grew up in such a system." One supervisor explained his work by saying, "You have to produce both healthy and able-bodied people and goods," and a colleague of his believed that her role was to "ensure that people develop, that they dare to take the extra step, they learn something, try to get them to think somewhat logically so that they don't get painful arms and legs, for then many of them will moan. That is what you have to nag into them." In this context, the staff magazine stated: "The role of a supervisor is to be a supportive resource .... The emphasis is on personal development; the medium is production."

A desirable profile for a supervisor seems to include empathy for the special problems that occupationally disabled are presumed to have. A manager of a Samhall wood company that employed five supervisors observed: "My supervisors must have an interest in the employees, an empathetic feeling." The corresponding qualifications as a manager were also emphasized by the Samhall CEO, who thought that it was important:

> to be a humanist. I wasn't a humanist when I began at Samhall, but have become one, for I have met so many of our employees, especially since I worked in a smaller town, then you meet many of the employees in the town ... and then you realize just how much the job means.

One supervisor felt that the occupationally disabled employees are usually "different than we that are normal," by being "very easy to talk to. They are kind of not ruffled socially." For similar reasons, another supervisor thought: "You see more of the person at a factory like this. Here, people display happiness, they display anger." Yet another supervisor reported, after describing the different groups of disabled that were employed at his work place (among others, "deaf people, alcoholics and addicts," as he called them), that "the problem is that many cannot be together in a normal way .... Often they quarrel about things we others regard as trifling matters and nothing worth paying attention to." A fellow supervisor at another work place had also had experienced this:

> The occupationally disabled make a mountain out of a molehill; it could be a trifling matter, a single component that causes them to dwell on the subject or just explode. For example, they don't have the ability to mince words, so they say what they think and then things can become a little crazy.

A colleague of his observed: "Many have mood swings, and it is up to them to control their tempers. When they get angry, they can be dangerous. But it can be pleasant too. You can get an infinite number of hugs, but also a great deal of telling off as well." He went on to say that the behavior of some of the employees was very unpredictable: "Suddenly, one morning they no longer greet you and can become completely enraged if you try talking to them, while another morning they can really seek contact." Another supervisor believed that much of the job of supervisor concerned "supporting them and keeping them apart when they quarrel," and one of his colleagues observed: "Working with the occupationally disabled is something special. It requires a lot of patience and clarity."

One supervisor felt that it was important to "be an amateur psychologist" in order to "understand people who are different," implying that, "it is important for new supervisors to study psychology before they start here at Samhall." A colleague of his agreed: "You have to be something of an amateur psychologist. Many of our personnel have psychosocial problems. You have to be able to read people to be able to prevent their incorrect treatment." Consequently, he thought: "You have to take time to talk to them, show them interest."

Caring by Demanding Less

Several supervisors reported that they always had to adjust to a "lower" level in their dealings with the occupationally disabled. One of them thought: "A lot is about adapting to the personnel. You have to hold back and make things simple and uncomplicated. You have to come down to their level." In their concern to simplify the work situation for the employees, "psychology is consequently one of the important aspects for us supervisors," one of them pointed out, and continued: "You have to break yourself down into different areas in order to get it to work. You have to be clear and distinct. You have to break down your language and your way of talking, use simple words and short sentences."

However, one supervisor thought, "The demands on the personnel are far too low," and another supervisor emphasized: "We are running a company here, not a daycare center." A nurse at Samhall's corporate health service believed, "Sometimes the requirements are too low. The employees think that they have a right to come to Samhall," and one supervisor observed that several of his employees "don't understand that they have to work to receive a wage." In a Swedish Radio report, one supervisor explained: "Many who start here come here with that idea, but actually it is a hard and good job. It is like any other job. It is not a daycare center any longer, as many call it when they first begin at Samhall." Even a government study bore this in mind: "The objective of Samhall is to produce goods and services that are in demand in the markets exposed to competition. Thus, it should be about real jobs, and not therapeutic operations."

Several supervisors experienced that they could not impose the same demands on the occupationally disabled employees as they could on employees in "normal companies," which one person working in personnel development at one of Samhall's so-called competence centers commented on by saying that the occupationally disabled employees had special needs. For that reason, "Samhall has developed a high degree of tolerance towards the employees, unlike other companies." One supervisor said: "It is a part of Samhall's culture. You can't force anyone to do anything. Imagine the headlines in the newspapers: 'The disabled forced to do this and that.'"

Another supervisor maintained that he had to be "very careful" all the time in his interaction with the occupationally disabled employees, and explained how he used to set about it:

> Normally, it is always like this: if I tell you, "You'll be able to do this, try it. I really believe you'll be able to do this," … you've been imbued with a positive feeling – "I will try. I will do it." Just hearing a positive sentence means a lot to a person who doesn't feel well.

In that respect, a behavioral scientist working in a staff function at Samhall thought that the division between the supervisors and the occupationally disabled employees, "creates different requirements. More requirements are placed on the supervisors than on the occupationally disabled." A company nurse believed: "Samhall demands very little. The occupationally disabled are free to muck things up. Nothing much happens. We pat them on the head – 'They are occupationally disabled.'" One supervisor explained: "We try to have a permissive and accepting attitude toward the occupationally disabled," and exemplified this by saying that they allowed things that other work places would find unacceptable, for example that someone "can be intoxicated. But if people are threatening, or simply dangerous, then we have to talk to them and calm them down."

At one work place there were a large number of jobs that needed to be carried out, but the work pace was generally calm due to frequent breaks, and even during the actual work time, several employees went round chatting with each other or sat reading newspapers or listening to the radio. The supervisors had no opinions about this, and one of them instead exhorted one of the employees, a highly educated immigrant working on sorting documents into different piles, "not to stress, for that will make you sick." At another work place, several of the occupationally disabled sat idle, had their hands on their work tables, went round talking on their cellular phones and looked out into the premises while some of their fellow workers in other work groups worked at the various tasks that had to be done. Sometimes, even with the same work group, several people worked while others sat reading daily newspapers or listening to the radio or absent-mindedly looking out of a window. At a work place meeting (an information meeting held periodically by the supervisor), several people sat sleeping, without any objections from the supervisor. A man suffering from Parkinson's disease, which affected his ability to speak, often sat just looking through a window and took no initiative to work, despite the fact that there were piles of paper on his table to be sorted. Again, his supervisor had no opinions about this behavior.

One of the occupationally disabled employees said: "The biggest difference here is the lack of responsibility. People get their wage regardless of whether or not they work." Another person, who had previous professional work experience before starting at Samhall, felt that Samhall was "very different." A third person said the work at Samhall was "calmer and more secure," and pointed out: "You can't be sacked here, and you don't have to work overtime." There were also employees who pointed out that Samhall was *not* any different to any other company, but often only as criticism. For example, one of them thought that people at Samhall "thought about money" just as much as people in other companies, and that "it's just as stressful here as anywhere else." One of his colleagues thought that they did not always get the special treatment people thought they ought to receive considering that they were ill and disabled: "It's no different here. We also do the same things normal people do."

A newly employed manager (who had previously worked as a manager at other company) had often posed the question of whether it was legitimate to impose the same demands on the occupationally disabled employees as employees at other work places. He reported, "I have really had to adapt my style of leadership," and that he had "to be much more careful since I am dealing with fragile individuals.

What I regard as trivialities can be immense for them." One site manager declared that at the beginning of his career, he "tried to make normal demands on the employees," but several of his subordinate supervisors, who had worked there for several years, had told him, "You can't do this because they are disabled." At this unit, they had "a major problem with drugs," and despite the objections of his fellow employees, he chose "to get to grips with this," whereas "things had previously been swept under the carpet." He gave the example of one of his employees who he "had managed to get into a treatment center," but "a lot of people here were against me for that." In his opinion: "Managers at Samhall are not encouraged to make normal demands on the employees. We have a lower standard here than at other companies."

Instructing the Disabled Employees

One supervisor felt that, on the whole, the occupationally disabled employees "need control personnel," especially for new types of work, such as when a new job arrives in a packaging workshop. Another supervisor pointed out that a new assignment was never handed over to the work team "in a democratic manner, which would have resulted in chaos." Thus, some supervisors were of the opinion that it was necessary for them to be clear in their direction of the employees. One supervisor thought that this stemmed from employees' "occupational disabilities and poor self-confidence." Another supervisor explained: "Since many of the occupationally disabled are apprehensive, clear guidelines are necessary." In this context, a head of an industrial enterprise emphasized: "Supervisors are needed. We need them to set the bar so that we don't have to discuss what applies."

As a supervisor, you had responsibility for "ensuring that the job is done correctly," one of them explained – for example, that the employees bent their knees when lifting heavy loads in the stores, that the mop was swept in a certain way while cleaning staircases, that washing machines were emptied according to a given routine, or that the production of a cabinet, a painter's roller, a certain meal or whatever was carried out in compliance with a given production routine. A supervisor who had worked for several other companies before coming to Samhall explained:

> Outside Samhall, you can hand out a job and know that it will be carried out, but I can never know if X here will do the same tomorrow as he did today, even if we are talking about carrying out the same job. The occupationally disabled forget things. They can get things into their heads. You have to keep a constant check, participate in the process itself.

A member of corporate management declared: "Our managers at Samhall have a more difficult target group to work with compared to that which exists in private industry. We have people who have not succeeded in the labor market by their own efforts. They have an occupational disability often requiring more instruction, more assistance." In general, a supervisor had "to be clear – often you think that the instructions you give are clear and the things you have talked about can only be done in one way, but often they [the employees] find other ways," one supervisor pointed out. In order to get people to behave in a certain way, "you can't play the boss and point with your whole hand," one supervisor said. Instead, "They should be allowed to say what they think and I should say what I think, and the whole idea is to get them to the point where they say what I had planned to say." This involved "asking the right questions, for example, 'How do you think this should be lifted?' And they say something, and then I ask, 'How does that feel?', and then they show me. These are the kinds of methods you have to use all the time."

Another supervisor believed: "If you really want someone to learn something, you have to control this. Thus, we very often ask, 'Have you done this and this?'" She declared that questioning was part of "the quality work, of ensuring that everything is done correctly." Some supervisors perceived that their primary role was *to lead* the development of the employees: "It's about getting them to do what we tell them to do. Then everything is okay," as one supervisor at a mechanical workshop pointed out.

Chapter 11
Sheltering from Reality's Complexity

A basic idea with an activation program like Samhall is that the occupationally disabled employees develop best by being offered a work environment that is sheltered from the normal requirements of the labor market. One supervisor declared: "It takes longer for our employees to do everything, and we take this into consideration in the production process." Another supervisor related about an unplanned order that had arrived and which had to be carried out immediately twice as quickly as was normal: "I and my colleagues [other supervisors] did this instead. The occupationally disabled would not have been able to manage this." In this context, a supervisor working with personnel who were on a staffing assignment for an external company reproached one of the Samhall personnel there for "trying to work as fast as [the company's] personnel" and "show that he was clever." He pointed out to the person, "You know that the stress isn't good for you," and then went and talked to the manager of the work place with a request to "reduce the pace of work ." However, the employee objected that he was not stressing, to which the Samhall supervisor commented: "You know what I'm saying is for your own good. You are here because previously you burned yourself out, and you could do that again."

The result of these and similar attitudes is that the work time for the execution of different jobs is often "adapted to the limitations of the employees," as one supervisor put it, which was also the case among Samhall's external staffing assignments, where Samhall's personnel "do not have to stress in the same way" as other personnel, according to one supervisor. Thus, at an external work place consisting of a storeroom, Samhall's personnel were allowed lesser quantities of work and several extra breaks. "Naturally, they don't like this," said one of the Samhall employees, referring to the rest of the personnel. However, the supervisor believed that the slower work tempo was necessary to look after the Samhall personnel's health.

A Slower Working Tempo

A newly employed supervisor at a Samhall unit remembered that he often became "frustrated" about the pace of work when he was new, but with time, he had "become more a part of this Samhall spirit. It is calmer and steadier, so now I feel a lot better." One of the occupationally disabled employees, a former cook who now worked on a completely different assignment at Samhall, said: "When I came here, I almost burst out laughing. When I was a cook, almost every minute was accounted for, but things are completely different here." Indeed, one supervisor thought that the overall atmosphere was "apathetic," and "everything here takes such a long time," but that one would have to adapt to this: "There is a reason for the existence of Samhall."

Several supervisors felt that, on the whole, the occupationally disabled employees were satisfied with working at a "pace that is adapted for them" (that is, a reduced pace), and where "complexity is adapted" (that is, where work assignments were simplified). "Sometimes you are surprised by some individuals who have such incredible job satisfaction in what they do, and which I personally wouldn't have been able to tolerate for more than two hours," a nurse at the corporate health service said. One member of corporate management declared of a work place where simple packing work was carried out: "Our employees working there are so overjoyed that they have a job."

However, one supervisor maintained that his personnel did not feel happy if "they are always being kept back," and that "they work best during temporary peaks [when there was more to do than usual]. Then they are like any other workers." This opinion was shared by one of his colleagues, who said that his personnel "worked like the devil" during a period when they were unusually understaffed due to vacations but they had the same amount of work. At a work place concerned with the distribution of food to retired citizens, two hours each morning were significantly 'more stressful' than the rest of the working day. One of the employees thought: "The early bird catches the worm. It is the best time of day." No one complained about the work pace. Instead, there was one person who pointed out: "After all, the retired citizens have to have their food in the morning." Each employee focused on his or her task of quickly sorting out the food so that it could then be distributed. To allow for the rapid pace, they did not sit down to work as they normally did. Instead, the benches were at standing height, which made it easier and quicker to package the goods and carry them out for distribution.

The distribution itself relied on the employees' own cars, where some employees acted as drivers and others ran or walked quickly up staircases to ring at the customers' doors or leave the food outside. When this was completed, a calm descended and simpler packaging jobs could take over (for example, sorting toys), but frequently they did not have anything else to do. Consequently, many wandered around in the corridors of the work place, sat reading the local newspaper or slept leaning up against a wall. One person felt this was "really tedious and boring." In that context, an occupationally disabled employee said: "The supervisors say that we have to work in peace and quiet, but I find it difficult to do that. I just want to push on."

At the work place involved with buying food for retired citizens for the home-help service from ordinary food stores described earlier, the supervisor said: "We try to make the job as close to reality as possible," and in so doing, challenged the prevailing sheltered environment within Samhall. At a certain time during the morning, the occupationally disabled usually took a fifteen-minute break to eat sandwiches and have coffee, after which they continued with their purchasing sessions. The drivers drove quickly around town, while their co-workers took the bags of food and delivered them to the customers, and when there were not too many items, they jogged along. Despite the rapid work pace in these groups compared to several other Samhall work places, they had among the lowest sick list figures in Samhall – approximately 7 percent.

However, not all the occupationally disabled employees appreciated a more intense working pace: "It's like any other company, stressful and hectic, and it shouldn't be like this here," as one of the employees expressed it. In that respect, one of his co-workers thought that his managers did not take into consideration the "disabilities and problems I have, which are the reason why I am here." Another employee wrote in a contribution in a book:

> It's like any other industry. Our new factory manager even goes down onto the shop floor and makes sure that his employees don't sit there doing nothing during five-minute breaks. That wouldn't be a good thing. Our purpose is to work as effectively as possible so that Samhall can take in as much money as possible. I believe the whole idea revolves around this concept! (Aulin, 2001)

In general, however, the job of the supervisor is to see that Samhall personnel are sheltered from the complexity of a 'normal' work pace in assignments, since the employees are occupationally *disabled*. A supervisor who visited a manufacturing industry where Samhall was being considered for a staffing assignment pointed out to two managers at the external work place: "The work must not be too difficult. Our employees are very fragile." Another supervisor described a firm where they had a staffing assignment where the employing company itself wanted to decide the pace of work for Samhall employees: "The company tried to optimize, and compared the time it took for the different employee categories. They failed to understand that our employees worked a lot slower." For this reason, another supervisor who had worked for several years hiring out Samhall personnel to other companies for staffing assignments believed that it was important that "the customer was made aware of the requirements of the occupationally disabled at an early stage," as the customers "often have difficulty understanding our special situation." In his opinion, "The customer cannot handle our personnel in the same way as other hired personnel. Our personnel require more care, for example a calmer work pace and more breaks."

Thus, in the case of staffing assignments at external work places, Samhall's supervisors regularly visited and went round and chatted with Samhall personnel, had coffee with them and held talks with the employer's personnel. The work place visits were motivated by the fact that they wanted to "look after our personnel," as one supervisor put it, but they also aimed to influence the employer, since: "Most of our customers have a hard time understanding our unique business. The personnel at other companies do not always understand that our employees are occupationally disabled, but treat them as if they were normal."

A nurse at a municipal home for the elderly which had personnel hired from Samhall said that there they had "adapted the assignments and working pace, and made everything simpler and more repetitive," compared to the assignments for the rest of the personnel, in consultation with the Samhall personnel's supervisor. She emphasized that the Samhall personnel did not do things that differed from other caregivers, but that they did them "on a smaller scale." For example, if a municipal worker took care of five residents, a Samhall employee only took care of two; if the municipality's personnel had a medical delegation for five elderly people, Samhall has a delegation for two, and so on. The nurse believed it was not possible to give the Samhall employees as many assignments as the ordinary personnel – it would be very stressful: "Real care is much more stressful than what we create for them." She emphasized that it was important to "choose simple tasks for Samhall people," and that it was about "carrying out fewer activities, but activities they can manage." A manager at another external work place where Samhall had personnel assumed that Samhall employees could not cope with the same work pace as the rest of the staff: "If you come here via Samhall, you know there is a reason. One can't give them too much to do." A Swedish Radio report about a number of Samhall employees working on an external staffing assignment observed: "At a work place like this, everyone has his or her personal problems and each person can work at his or her own pace. That is why they have ten janitors, where a normal company would have four."

At several external work places, personnel from Samhall may work side by side with personnel from other staffing companies and with the same work assignments, the only difference being that there are more Samhall personnel: "Here we use two or three persons where a normal company would only use one," the supervisor of a work team explained. The same applied to a street cleaning and park administration concern, where there were more Samhall personnel than there were from other companies. Certainly, Samhall "may not compete when it comes to price. However, the one thing we can compete with, for example when negotiating external cleaning assignments, is more personnel," a member of corporate management declared, concluding: "In many assignments, we can provide a few more hands."

A manager at an external work place experienced Samhall personnel as a "closely knit group." Another manager at another work place complained: "They send us one idiot after the other, but we have no chance of having any effect on this." At another work place, they wanted to change these routines: "So far, it has been the Samhall personnel who have taught each other, and for this reason there have been lots of mistakes. We want control over this so that things are done in the correct way." This opinion was shared by a supervisor at another work place: "We would like to have Samhall people obeying our rules so that we don't differentiate between man and beast, as it were." Often, the Samhall employees worked by themselves at the external work places where Samhall had staffing assignments, physically separated from the rest of the permanent or temporary personnel.

At a meeting between two supervisors from and two representatives of a customer who had already hired personnel from Samhall and who was thinking about extending this, one of the Samhall representatives declared that there were many "prejudices" about Samhall employees, that "they are only wheelchair-bound or mentally retarded and nutcases," but according to him, the truth was: "Our personnel are capable as long as you provide them with a fixed framework." He went on to explain a little more about state subsidy for additional costs, which is supposed to compensate Samhall for the fact that the personnel "cannot work as hard as others" and for the fact that when it comes to new jobs that Samhall personnel were not used to, it "takes our employees a little longer to get started." The Samhall supervisor explained that sickness rates were also "somewhat higher than normal, but then we are carrying the can at staffing," and explained that "people apply to Samhall to avoid the tough requirements of the labor market."

His colleague added that the customer's personnel had to think about "giving our employees a lot of praise," as: "Our employees have poor self-confidence. They need more assistance than others." One Samhall supervisor working with staff in another part of the country declared that she often visited the customers where Samhall already had personnel or planned staffing in order to tell them about "the road to employment at Samhall" and "the special qualifications our employees have owing to a complicated history." Generally speaking, she meant that the customer had to "understand the point of Samhall," and that "our employees are a little slower and cannot successfully tackle things that are too difficult." In that respect, she felt: "Managers at the customers' [premises] must be well familiarized with what Samhall stands for in order for things to function."

One manager working with Samhall employees at an external work place related:

> One has to change as a person. I have to be a little milder. I can't set the same requirements that I normally would. I have learnt to listen and receive information about a person's background in order to be able to handle him/her in the correct way. With our own employees [non-Samhall personnel], I don't need to worry about such things. I only have to give orders.

A manager at another work place where Samhall had also hired out staff declared that Samhall's personnel "are not given heavier jobs like lifting or more advanced assignments, such as working with computers. You have to think about their disability, it doesn't suit them."

An occupationally disabled employee who worked in a care home for the elderly together with municipally employed personnel observed: "Samhall employees are given a month to learn the job, while those employed by the municipality have only three days for this." The supervisor for the Samhall personnel had obtained extra internal funds for this as part of a project to adapt the work environment for Samhall employees at work places where staffing assignments took place. This was also to compensate for Samhall personnel's need not "to stress in the same way" as municipal personnel, as the supervisor put it. A manager at a company that hired Samhall personnel said: "Samhall personnel should not have to stress. As soon as things become stressful, they do not function. Samhall has told us that we must offer a stress-free environment." In one of Samhall's annual reports, a representative for a client company declared: "We hire Samhall personnel for the same types of assignments carried out by our own personnel. ... The only difference is the work rate, since individuals that come from Samhall have to work at a calmer pace."

For this reason, one supervisor believed that Samhall:

> would not be able to compete with other companies without subsidies [from the state]. We would get no assignments [from customers]. We can't get assignments with people who don't have the energy to go back to work after a vacation and where it takes two weeks before everyone is back in place. Normal work places don't have this kind of situation.

This experience was shared by a member of corporate management, who had worked in private industry during the earlier part of his career:

> I can look back on my own experiences when the supervisors [at the companies previously worked for] acquired new personnel. Then, it was a question of a half-day introduction out on the line. This is not what it's like here. Here, it takes a couple of weeks, perhaps a couple of months of introduction, and we have the patience and the resources to train people to get started – others companies don't have this!

He thought that "very few" of the occupationally disabled employees would be able to get started with a job in the same way as in other companies, saying: "For example, take someone who has come here for socio-medical reasons and who has now decided to 'give up the bottle.' It's obvious that this person wouldn't be able to do this. He would soon be back to his old tricks again."

Similar assumptions about the capacity and behavior of the occupationally disabled are reflected in the distrust exhibited by a number of supervisors toward the occupationally disabled. When two people employed in a cleaning team reported that they had cleaned eight stairwells in 90 minutes, their supervisor said: "That's impossible. They have cheated." During subsequent telephone contacts with the group leader for the cleaners, it turned out that the work had been carried out in a satisfactory way. Another occupationally disabled person working on a staffing assignment reported: "They [the supervisors] had said that this is a four-hour job, but I finished it in half the time, and when I tell them this, they don't believe me. Instead, I hear that I am stressed and need to wind down." One supervisor at another work place said: "Unfortunately, we don't have any easy assignment here," which he thought was a problem since "many of our employees cannot handle multi-operational machines." He contrasted this with a "normal factory," where the personnel could work on several operations at a time, saying: "People here are only able to cope with one thing at a time."

Chapter 12
Developing in a Disabled World

Occupationally disabled employees at Samhall work in an organization that assumes that they *are* occupationally disabled, with all the special need and preferences that characterize such a group. For example, in most issues of Samhall's staff magazine there are articles that are variations on the themes of illness, disability, addiction and problems, often with reports about individual employees. Even in the annual reports, in advertising brochures and so on, employees are the focus of personal reports which detail the problems which are said to have led to their employment at Samhall. For example, in one issue of the magazine, an employee said: "Since I have a motor disorder, I try to sit as much a possible, and that works well," or as the reporter described it: "When Ingela moves, she supports herself using a crutch." An interview with an employee in another issue began with: "Since I have the disability of Down's Syndrome, I need to be able to work at my own pace. I've always been able to do this at Samhall." A report about a golf tournament in which one of Samhall's employees participated again focused on the employee's difficulties: "Most of my problems are on my right side. My right hand only functions as a support when I hit the ball. I limp on my right leg, and this affects my balance and golf swing." An employee at Samhall's telephone switchboard was presented as, "Lena has a past history of working with the care of the elderly, but her back didn't stand up to such heavy work," and in a report from one factory, a man said: "We can alternate jobs and do the things we can cope with from the point of view of our injuries. All of us have more or less pain somewhere."

Different stories in the staff magazine also reinforce the view the surrounding world has of Samhall employees as sick, disabled and generally injured. One article, "Functionally disabled are described as abnormal on Swedish Television," maintained that: "This is unusual with TV programs that depict persons with functional disorders as active citizens," and "often the functionally disabled are presented as abnormal." In another report in which schoolchildren were interviewed about their perceptions of the occupationally disabled, it was made clear that in their eyes, occupationally disabled people were physically and mentally limited.

Furthermore, the staff magazine frequently provides information on appropriate literature, which the occupationally disabled are encouraged to familiarize themselves with and which cover such themes as disability, functional disorder, sickness and so forth. Normally, it is emphasized that the information is presented in "a simple manner that is easy to understand," which is said to be important for the occupationally disabled. For example, one article gave tips about readability on the Web, with a special recommendation for a homepage offering an easy-to-read newspaper. In another article, there was information about "Democracy in easy-to-read Swedish," and there were tips about a "book about democracy" that "is especially aimed at persons with mental retardation." It stated: "There are 4,000 people working at Samhall with intellectual functional disorders .... The book *Take Part and Decide* has been written for them." Another article carried recommendations partly about a book about the childhood and adolescence of a blind boy that was characterized by "penalization, constant abuse and victimization, both from children and adults," and partly about a person who "is told that he is suffering from incurable cancer" and "as a reader, you are almost able to follow Lars right up to his last breath."

A Disabled Self?

Many occupationally disabled employees refer to illnesses and other problems when talking about themselves, for example by introducing themselves with, "I'm dyslectic," "I have a problem with my back," "I have an ulcer" or "I have heel spurs." A highly educated immigrant suffering from multiple sclerosis who now worked at one of Samhall's factories on packaging assignments said: "This sickness has destroyed my life, my dreams, my career." Another employee who had difficulties in speaking due to a car accident used to hand over a copy of a magazine report to visitors at his work place. The report had the heading: "This is how my life was changed. All my dreams about my future were wiped out in a second!"

Aulin (2001) pointed out that she had not received the aids she felt she needed, and in the same book several other employees criticized Samhall for not showing sufficient consideration for their injuries and problems. A mother of six who had previously worked as an official within a local authority but who had subsequently been unemployed for many years and who now worked in a mechanical workshop at Samhall said: "I feel great. I will never be unemployed again." The work entailed heavy lifting and twisting phases of steel components. She emphasized that she had problems with her shoulders: "This is documented. It is in my papers. This is why I am here."

A Swedish Radio report covered the work assignments at one of Samhall's laundry facilities, which included ironing hundreds of pieces of clothing per day. Several of the women interviewed specified that the reason they were working there was that their worn-out shoulders and backs made it impossible for them to work on the open labor market. The reporter wondered whether ironing was suitable for someone with worn-out shoulders as their occupational disability, but, referring to one of the supervisors and to a member of Samhall's corporate management who were also interviewed, stated: "Well-being, variety and the possibilities of being able to control one's own work are more important for health than what they actually do." A woman who sat picking up iron screws and holding metal rails all day said: "I've been on the other side [outside Samhall], but I couldn't stay there since I had a nickel allergy."

Another woman working on a Samhall staffing assignment in a food store declared that she had problems with her back. The work entailed filling one basket per customer with such perishable foodstuffs as dairy products, flour and sugar, carrying them through a large food store, and then re-packing the goods into food bags, which were then distributed to the customers. This involved loading and unloading packages from cars and carrying the food bags up and down stairwells. She explained: "I can't sit down. That's why I have a painful back." Earlier, she had worked as a seamstress and had sat down all day, but the textile and clothing industry where she lived had closed down, and eventually she was made redundant.

Several supervisors encouraged the personnel in work groups to "talk about their problems." At a work place meeting, one supervisor suggested that each working week should commence with a ten-minute discussion about "the difficulties you are carrying around with you," and that the allocation of the work for the day should be based on this discussion, where "Those that don't feel all that bad this week can do a little more than those that feel worse." This was already a routine at another work place, and the supervisor declared: "Several people need someone to talk to in the mornings when they have problems at home." Some supervisors took part in the discussions, and one of them often told a person who was sad about a personal issue: "You are really good," and "I know you can do this." Another supervisor felt that regular meetings of this kind were important to bring out "if there is anything that doesn't feel right" for any of the personnel. He linked this to the individual's private life during one of these meetings: "If you don't feel well here and are unhappy, it will affect your families. Therefore, it is important that everyone speaks up about why they are here and what problems are behind this."

One supervisor emphasized how important it was for occupationally disabled employees to be "honest about their problems" in front of each other, declaring: "The most difficult thing is our obligation to secrecy. We [supervisors] cannot openly talk about the problems of [occupationally disabled] colleagues." The Swedish Law about the Obligation to Secrecy in Samhall states:

> Anyone who takes part in or has taken part in operations which through the production of goods and services strives towards achieving meaningful and stimulating work for the occupationally disabled may not without authorization reveal what he or she has learned about an occupationally disabled employee's personal circumstances.

However, in order to circumvent this rule, "We try to encourage our employees to be open with each other. We have mutually decided that we should not conceal our problems," as one of the supervisors put it.

In spite of this, one of the employees thought that at the work place in question, "The manager never asks me how I feel, even if he knows that I am sick." A co-worker declared: "Samhall doesn't care how you feel," relating that earlier, they had had so-called personnel counselors who visited Samhall's work places "who had time to work with our problems." Another employee wrote in a contribution in a book: "In my job, they can't even afford to have a nurse on site more than every other week, despite the fact that we are 200 people!" At another work place, one of the occupationally disabled employees observed: "We are used to talking about how we feel. If I feel bad, I say so, and then the others know that it's okay with a break." Another employee declared: "We are open about our problems in the work team. We have to be. We are talking about complete trust." In a Samhall information CD-ROM aimed at supervisors, "rules for communication" in connection with "work team meetings" were taken up, in which it was emphasized:

> Rules for content are about what can be discussed, what is on the borderline or what may not be discussed. Things are different in different situations. There are subjects that you can talk about with fellow workers, but that you can't discuss with your mother – and vice versa. Naturally, the more subjects and feelings allowed, the better the quality of communication. Often it's good for communication at work to have more personal issues among the permitted topics of discussion, such as the family, hobbies, leisure-time activities and feelings.

Samhall's staff magazine aimed at all employees often features articles dealing with how to identify problems in co-workers in order to relate to them (in their capacity as occupationally disabled) more effectively. One report, "A capricious disability," dealt with stammering. The report had two aims: partly to ascertain that stammering *is* a disability, and to emphasize that a person who stammers is disabled, and partly to provide advice and tips for employees about how stammering colleagues can be identified and treated. The article pointed out that "stammering is a very capricious disability" which "can become a social disability," since "many people who stammer withdraw, become silent. ... Stammering sometimes affects both self-confidence and the quality of life." Consequently, the attitudes in one's environment are considered important: "Colleagues can give a person who stammers time. Do not fill in those words you believe he or she will say. If you are unsure, it's best to ask the person who stammers how he or she should be treated."

In another report about epilepsy, one of the Samhall employees talked about "what it's like to live with the illness" and how one can recognize an epileptic. She explained how she often had minor epileptic attacks and fell down, but could quickly get up again: "Since I scrape my knees quite a lot when I fall down, I have received knee-guards from the corporate health service," which also made it easier for those around her to understand that she had problems. She thought that one should be open about one's epilepsy: "I have always told people around me about my illness. It's more secure, for both them and me." The report also took up the issue of "What is epilepsy?" and how an epileptic is expected to behave: "An attack can be frightening for someone who has never seen one before, but it is relatively harmless." Thus, the article encouraged people to "talk about their epilepsy with supervisors, fellow workers, relatives and friends." This was considered to have several benefits, such as "people understand you and your situation" and "you meet more people."

One supervisor reported that employees often "voluntarily tell me about their problems, and this demonstrates their trust for me as their boss." Another supervisor explained that the knowledge acquired from employees' case files was complemented by ongoing discussions at work about the individual's situation at work and in life. She believed that to be a good supervisor who can contribute to the development of employees, "it is important to acquire a fundamental knowledge of the personnel, which requires that I work with them for a long time. You have to get a handle on the personnel." She gave the example of one of the employees "she talked with a lot," since "she had problems with her son and other things." During most work days they sat down at the coffee table together with the other personnel to "talk through what has happened," as the supervisor explained, and it concluded with the supervisor giving the employee a hug.

Another supervisor said that he always tried to put himself in the employee's "overall life situation" by means of discussions during personal development talks or on other occasions, and exemplified this with a person "who had not had contact with relatives for more than twenty years" as an explanation of why the person "felt so bad." In exceptional cases, some supervisors also had contact with employees' doctors and parents, with whom they could discuss problems and needs, and doctors and parents could also contact the supervisors.

In a number of meetings in which work group members were encouraged to talk about their individual problems and limitations under the guidance of the supervisor, a member of Samhall's corporate health service would take part – a behavioral scientist or a corporate nurse. One of them said:

> Many times I have been surprised that the occupationally disabled are not more concerned about their privacy. They talk openly about their problems. I think they should probably maintain a certain degree of privacy. Naturally, some people should know, but not everyone should know what has happened in my life, about how terrible things have been.

However, an information CD-ROM distributed by Samhall aimed at supervisors pointed out:

> It is important not to lose sight of the overall views of people at work. It is not possible to cater for one dimension and lose sight of the rest. For a person with a functional disorder, his or her entire existence must function in order for life to be tolerable: travel to work, the work environment both physically and psycho-sociologically, including one's private life.

For this reason, it was assumed that a comprehensive analysis of each employee's life situation based on his or her occupational disability was needed.

The focus on problems in work groups and between co-workers during coffee breaks and at lunchtime was not only about creating a forum for the exchange of experiences between the occupationally disabled, but also about creating an arena for increased understanding for their respective situation *as* occupationally disabled, and consequently greater competence in treating each other as occupationally disabled individuals. One supervisor explained that it was very important for personnel to "understand each other's problems and disabilities" and to "learn to take these into consideration." Another supervisor thought that personnel "must think disability" when they interact with each other, and "adapt their behavior for everyone who has a disability." In this context, one supervisor said that it was important to "teach people to show consideration for each other's problems."

At some work places there were posters or documents describing how to recognize different types of disability and how one should relate to these. At one work site where some hearing-impaired people worked, there was a document posted: "Seven good pieces of advice when talking to a hearing-impaired person." Among other things, this stated:

> Make sure that you have the attention of the hearing-impaired person. He or she must both see hear and see when you talk – Try to get eye contact! … Never hide behind a newspaper or similar. Never talk with your hand in front of your mouth or with something in your mouth. … Speak clearly – not too quickly. Repeat if necessary. … Avoid unnecessary noise – turn down the radio and sound sources. Try to maintain a calm environment.

In work places, hearing-impaired employees often worked together and communicated via sign language. In interaction with fellow workers who were not hearing-impaired, their behavior changed – avoiding eye contact, looking down at the floor, nodding abruptly. From having behaved as "non-deaf" in their interaction with other hearing-impaired people, except that they used sign language to communicate, they began to behave in a way that the surrounding world expected of deaf people – signaling with gestures to their ears that they could not hear, at which non-hearing-impaired colleagues changed their behavior and began talking more precisely, using sweeping gestures.

Even in the work groups Samhall employees belonged to in external staffing assignments – for example, within care homes for the elderly, in which employees from other organizations were included – the Samhall employees were encouraged to talk about their limitations. A supervisor for such assignments pointed out how important it was for Samhall employees to talk about their problems, as otherwise, there "can be problems in relations with them. People know that they come from Samhall and so they expect that they have problems and should relate why they are there." The supervisor explained that it was "extra difficult to tell people about things that aren't visible externally, but they have to say something. Of course, people wonder, 'How will things turn out? How will they be able to manage?'"

Within and between the work groups, people sometimes talked about each other as "muppets" (as in *The Muppet Show*). The concept was accepted and even used by supervisors when referring to occupationally disabled people. One supervisor believed that this concept came from the time when Samhall "only employed the motor-disabled and mentally retarded. But that's not the case any longer. Now we accept all types of people. It is no longer a muppet workshop." A new employee had heard from her friends, "What, are you going to start at the muppet's workshop?", which had upset her, she said. In spite of this, she herself talked about some of her fellow workers at the work place as "muppets." Several occupational disabled individuals felt that Samhall was branded a "handicap factory." One middle-aged employee who had worked at Samhall for a few years explained: "I often sit thinking, 'I have to be stupid,' since I'm working here. I never thought like this before I began at Samhall. But since I am together with muppets all day, perhaps I have become an idiot myself." A colleague of his reflected: "In a way, you feel that you're secure here. You have a secure job, and if you work outside Samhall, it's easy to get fired. On the other hand, I'm healthy, but I work with sick people all day. Sometimes I ask myself how this is affecting me."

A newly employed occupationally employee declared:

> In the beginning, I tried to be normal, but in time you start to act stupid in order to be able to cope. It's kind of like a game for each other. I often have to sink the level of others in order to be able to work with them. You have to be able to express yourself in their way. There is a risk that you can switch over, that some day you will become like them yourself.

An occupationally disabled man working in a packaging workshop was critical toward "mixing different personnel groups," maintaining, "they mix us up with mentally retarded," which, according to him, entailed that: "We that are not so sick must adapt to those that are really sick. Eventually, we may also become sick."

Experiencing Disability

The fact that many at Samhall experience problems, feel bad, feel ill and so on can be illustrated with sickness rate statistics. According to recent Samhall annual reports, on average, sickness rate are at 20 percent, and in certain units they can amount to 30 percent, which should be compared with the average for companies in Sweden of approximately 3–5 percent. In one of the annual reports, the explanation for the relatively high sickness rate at Samhall was said to be the fact that "Samhall employees have functional disorders that can increase sensitivity for different kinds of stresses in and outside of the job," thus pointing out that "as in previous years, employees at Samhall report more occupational injuries than employees in other companies. Labor-related illnesses have increased during recent years and are at a higher level than in the rest of industry." This was explained "in part by the fact that different functional disorders increase the risk for injuries, in part by the fact that employees at Samhall many times can have greater difficulty in assessing risks and understanding instructions." Furthermore, it was maintained that current reorganizations at Samhall were a reason for sick-listings: "Major restructuring has taken place within Samhall during recent years, which has led to many employees ending up in unfamiliar situations, thereby increasing the risk of injuries."

A manager at a company in which Samhall had a staffing assignment related that there was a higher frequency of absence due to illness among the occupationally disabled than among other hired personnel, despite the fact that Samhall staff had simpler assignments and had more members in their work teams, as well as the right to more breaks, in accordance with the agreement between the company and Samhall. Samhall had also sent a human engineer there to ensure that the working environment was suitable for the employees. In a similar way, Samhall's operational policy was emphasized:

> The majority of Samhall's employees are people with functional disorders who often are very sensitive to work environment risks such as stress, physical pressure and the affects of chemicals. Therefore, Samhall has higher demands for not only the psycho-social work environment but also the physical work environment compared to other companies.

The manager at an external work place in which Samhall had placed staff did not believe that the Samhall personnel were more prone to illness than the rest of the hired staff, but felt that the job security the Samhall personnel enjoyed made them more likely to report sick: "They can't be fired. You wonder what their ambitions are. The worst thing that can happen is that they are relocated from a place they like."

On the whole, supervisors did not feel that the high sickness rates at Samhall were anything out of the ordinary, since Samhall personnel *were* sick and disabled: "That is why they are here," as one supervisor put it. In general, there was an attitude among the supervisors that it was impossible to influence the problems and limitations the personnel were suffering from: "Sick-listings are around 20 percent, and we can't do anything about that," one of them said. Thus, one supervisor had a "philosophy," as he called it, of always "overstaffing" the external assignments for which he was responsible, as there "is always a risk that someone has reported sick." An occupationally disabled employee said: "Samhall understands us. They aren't so strict. Here, you can be on the sick list for a long time and not lose your job, or it's okay to take breaks more frequently. The supervisors understand this." One supervisor thought that the fact that the personnel were often home because they "felt bad" was not strange, explaining: "Many of our employees have problems, thus it's only natural that they often feel bad and don't come to work." An occupationally disabled employee who had worked in private industry for many years, but who had been sick-listed due to an injury caused by crushing and was now employed at Samhall, pointed out: "There is a 20 percent absence due to illness here, but nobody is bothered about this."

Chapter 13
Exiting as "Non-disabled"

The ultimate goal of Samhall, as with any activation program in the modern welfare state, is that the client's employability is strengthened. Hence, ending one's career at Samhall and beginning employment with a "regular" organization is the ultimate goal of Samhall's activities, and according to Samhall, the ultimate proof that the company's activation program works. At Samhall, this is called "transition." An information CD-ROM for Samhall's supervisors states:

> Transitions are a business goal for Samhall. They can also constitute an important individual goal for the individual employee. It is an important task for Samhall to stimulate its employees in different ways to try a transition. A knowledge of the surrounding work and curiosity as well as support from Samhall are important ... before a transition, during the period of practice and at the new work place.

According to its agreement with the state, Samhall aims to achieve transitions amounting to 5 percent of existing staff.

"The organized transition process," as it is called at Samhall, consists of a number of practices, ceremonies and procedures aimed at "guaranteeing the same serious approach at the termination of employment as at its beginning, regardless of the reason for the transition," which is the reason why the transition process is surrounded by organizational rules and routines that are expressions of the rehabilitation efforts. The formal responsibility for transitions lies with the employee's supervisor at Samhall and the NEO, in accordance with the collaboration agreement, as was pointed out on the Samhall internal Website:

> Our organizations have a mutual responsibility for providing the Samhall employee with opportunities for a transition to employment with another employer. On the part of the Samhall company, this involves everything from preparatory and motivation-augmenting measures to supporting and following up the employee after the transition to another employer. When the efforts and forms of support provided by the National Employment Office are deemed necessary, the National Employment Office is also afforded a responsibility for contributing toward bringing about a transition. An important point of departure is that all employees that are prepared for a transition are reported and registered as applicants for an exchange at the National Employment Office.

The Formal Process

Supervisors have responsibility for deciding whether occupationally disabled employees are ready for a transition, based on their experience of their development. The supervisors then contact the NEO so that together with an administrative official there, they can decide on a suitable work place outside Samhall. A government study that carried out an interview survey among Samhall's occupationally disabled employees with the aim of mapping Samhall's transition work posed the question, "Have you ever during recent years talked to your immediate superior about what will happen with you in the future?", which hinted at the significance of supervisors in realizing transitions.

An NEO administrative official was of the opinion that "those people who succeeded in transferring" were those that had "been observed" by their supervisor "for a long time." According to a Samhall document, the process is initiated when "the employee and his or her immediate superior are in agreement during the personal development discussion that the employee is *prepared for a transition* (both can and wants to do it)." This form contains personal information about the employee, "development efforts during the time at Samhall" in the form of "training courses" and "work experience," as well as "current work qualifications at Samhall," where a "description of an occupational disability" and "need for possible preparatory efforts and/or support in the working situation" should be filled in. The form should be signed by the supervisor and the employee, whose signature confirms that "I [the occupationally disabled individual] herewith approve that the National Employment Office may be informed of the current report from Samhall's corporate health service," as well as the contents of other documents in the employee's case file.

Among other things, the responsibility of the NEO for transitions concerns offering a prospective employer a wage allowance during the first year of employment, which usually amounts to a 50–70 percent state subsidy of the wage of the former Samhall employee (this presupposes that the person continues to be coded as occupationally disabled, which is an NEO requirement for granting a wage allowance). One supervisor at Samhall emphasized: "We are forced to pay out wage allowances since the occupationally disabled do not have the same capacity as healthy people." Consequently, "Wage allowances are central for our transitions," another supervisor at Samhall pointed out, which was confirmed by an NEO administrative official, who thought: "There is a difference between working in a sheltered work place [Samhall] and at a normal work place. The occupationally disabled person may need extra instruction and the like," which would thus justify a wage allowance.

One supervisor thought that the wage subsidy was important in interesting an employer in taking on a Samhall employee, emphasizing that "The system protects both the employer and the employee." This was also maintained in a research report from 2001, which established that employers regarded wage subsidies as important in offering employment to an occupationally disabled person. The employer "gets some protection against the fact that the employee may not produce as well as others," and the employee "does not have to produce as much thanks to the subsidy, and this provides some security," a supervisor explained.

In a CD-ROM distributed by Samhall containing information for supervisors, one passage emphasized with regard to the transition work:

> A company's primary task is to produce goods and services and to be profitable. Thus, companies do not normally employ people with functional disorders for charitable reasons, but to satisfy the company's own needs. In the event of impaired capacity, the employer can apply for various labor market policy contributions [such as wage allowances].

The same CD-ROM refers to a study about "the view of company management on the functionally disabled," and states: "The study shows that economic aspects have great importance for the employment of a disabled person."

The cooperation document between Samhall and the NEO regarding transitions points out that the process should be based on so-called "three-party collaboration," where officials at the NEO, the occupationally disabled employee and the supervisor at Samhall pursue the process together. However, in practice, it is often only the NEO administrative official and the supervisor at Samhall who have direct contact, while the occupationally disabled employee only has communication with his or her supervisor. An administrative official at the NEO explained that they do not allow occupationally disabled employees to make contact on their own initiative for the purpose of bringing about a transition if their supervisors are unaware of this: "We decided not to approve this. It must go through the supervisor. It is not possible without the consent of the supervisor."

During the three-party discussion which includes the occupationally disabled employee, the employee may talk about his or her experiences and what sort of work he or she would like to do outside Samhall: "The person tells me he would rather work at cleaning, storeroom work or in a restaurant," an NEO administrative official explained, but most often, "There is nothing written down about how they function in the different kinds of work and we would really like to know this when trying to place these different persons." Another NEO official was of the opinion that "it's not realistic" to merely rely on what the employee said, and therefore felt that the supervisor was a more reliable indicator of the person's work capacity. Yet another NEO official pointed out, however, that "Samhall shows us which persons are ready for a transition, but it's not always certain that this tallies." Each case a supervisor judges suitable for a transition does not always result in one: "Sometimes the supervisor has to compromise," an NEO administrator declared, since the NEO official also makes judgments about suitability.

Indeed, it would be theoretically possible for an occupationally disabled employee at Samhall to look for a job on his or her own initiative, without the involvement of the NEO and supervisor, and eventually find employment outside Samhall. In practice, this is probably impracticable, since it is likely that a potential employer would require a wage supplement in order to hire a former Samhall employee, as well as assuming that the potential employee was disabled, injured or generally suffering from problems. Furthermore, as in any other company, authority or similar employment, Samhall employees cannot simply hand in their notice and expect economic support from the unemployment benefit fund, which only caters for people who are laid off involuntarily. Even if the person in question was able to manage such a situation economically without unemployment benefits, he or she would probably be regarded as an especially problematic case by the NEO if he or she made contact with it while attempting to arrange a new job.

Redundancy due to lack of work is something Samhall employees do not have to reckon with, since up to now the company has never applied this. Not making people with occupational disabilities redundant when there is a lack of work at Samhall is something of a "holy cow," and is thought to create a good base for the activation of the employees by offering them a secure and stable work environment. Thus, in reality, Samhall employees enjoy lifetime employment in the form of posts with conditional tenure where redundancy due to lack of work is not an option. A government study observed that "Since Samhall was founded, no employee with an occupational disability has been made redundant due to lack of work," even if this is formally possible. This possibility "is simply not *used*," the study pointed out. For this reason, "you are almost a serf at Samhall," one of the occupationally disabled employees declared.

Appropriate Jobs for the Activated Post-disabled Person

A manager at Samhall working on transitions felt that occupationally disabled employees are often suited to "the somewhat simpler jobs" on the labor market, such as being someone's "man Friday": "I can say to an employer, 'Why are you, an economist, making coffee when one of my employees can do it for you?'" One supervisor explained:

> When people have been recruited from Samhall, we are talking about assignments that do not require a high degree of competence. We are talking about jobs as storeroom workers, janitors, receptionists, assembly workers, often man Fridays, someone to just look after a house. The occupationally disabled can't manage sales, often they are not extrovert enough. They can't deal with things that require more competence, such as personal economy, so we are talking about simpler assignments.

Samhall's internal Website, under the "Job Links" tab, publicizes current jobs suitable for transitions. On one occasion, the following services in the Stockholm area were available:

- administrator;
- general office duties;
- man Friday;
- man Friday/stores;
- auto detailing;
- bookkeeping/accounting;
- café assistant;
- café service;
- janitor/assistant;
- shopping cart handling;
- stores, real estate work;
- stores work;
- assistant, man Friday;
- assistant in restaurant;
- musician;
- reconditioner/man Friday;
- fairy-story teller;
- personnel for waiting at table;
- carpenters, welders, store assistants;
- stableman;
- stable services;
- janitor/man Friday;
- hostess/host;
- handling of recyclables/returnables.

In a report in the staff magazine, there was a story about one of the employees who got a job at McDonald's after eighteen years at Samhall. The job did not involve working in the kitchen or serving customers at the counter, which are the most common assignments at McDonald's and which are often occupied by schoolchildren, immigrants and people with a low level of education. Instead, the occupationally disabled person cleaned the restaurant area, toilets and kitchen, as well as replenishing napkins and straws in the racks in the premises. Several photos illustrated the man's industrious work cleaning tables with a cloth, and the text said: "The tables have been dried, there are no packages lying around after untidy guests, the chairs are placed tidily and properly awaiting new customers."

In Samhall's CD-ROM directed toward supervisors, an argument that is maintained as a motivation for external employers to employ Samhall employees is that it provides "goodwill" and "increased value." It points out, "a company that deliberately encourages recruitment of persons with functional disorders and emphasizes this condition strengthens the increased value with respect to the customers," which is exemplified by McDonald's: "A little more than a quarter of McDonald's 189 restaurants have one or more employees with a functional disorder, some without a wage allowance: 'Working at McDonalds doesn't only imply selling hamburgers, but also strikes a blow for human equality.'"

A Samhall staff member who was responsible for transitions for a number of Samhall work places declared that "95 percent of those leaving here do not continue with the work they did at Samhall," which is in line with the conception within Samhall that the company is not a vocational training work place, but an arena for activating people in general terms. A government study of Samhall determined: "In the first place, it is not primarily a specific occupational competence that is the objective of employment at Samhall, but more a general working life qualification." A supervisor at a Samhall mechanical workshop where most of the employees fabricated sheet metal to produce metal cabinets – including cutting, bending, welding, milling, assembling and painting – explained that most of the transitions from his work place had not resulted in jobs within the same industry, but had led to jobs like "janitors at schools, conference facilities, museums."

A person in charge of transitions for several Samhall work places pointed out that activation "is about being able to get started, being punctual, getting up in the morning, going to work, doing a job during the day, different kinds of instructions. Some people can't read, can't write. It may be about social training, about being together with different people." What Samhall produces, and consequently the occupational skills that can be acquired by employees, is of secondary importance to the idea of providing the occupationally disabled with employment, which was emphasized in a government study: "According to a government bill, the purpose of Samhall's activities is to guarantee the occupationally disabled employee's right to a paid job. Thus, the production of goods and services is not of significance in itself."

Training as "Non-disabled"

Most of the time, transitions are preceded by so-called "external practice periods," where the Samhall employee is allowed to serve at a work place for approximately one month, the wage being paid by Samhall. One supervisor thought that the period of practice was "something we should work more with. I have often thought, 'How they have grown' when they have returned." Ideas about practice adhere to the internal perception that Samhall is a world unto itself, partly separated from "reality," and where the periods of practice are geared to teaching occupationally disabled employees how to behave in the "real world." Sometimes practice is even used at work places outside Samhall without an eye to this leading to a transition, but simply to provide the employee with "work training," as one supervisor explained, "to be in a real-life situation," as another supervisor thought, and "to provide the person with fresh air," as a third supervisor put it. One supervisor emphasized that other work places were "the real-life situation," and that it was important that Samhall's employees could practice there "and work in a real environment." One supervisor explained, "In theory, Samhall should mirror reality on the outside," but that "in practice, this doesn't work with our employees," because he and the other supervisors felt that the employees were unable to tackle flexitime, "which is normal practice at most other work places, but doesn't work here."

The trainee post is confirmed in a written agreement with the employer, and covers either a "job trial prior to employment" or "other practice." Among other things, the agreement states: "Wages are paid by Samhall during the period of practice. The period of practice is covered by labor market insurance and liability insurance through Samhall." On one occasion, a supervisor had gone with a Samhall employee to a restaurant which had said it was willing to discuss the possibility of a trainee post. The employee himself had made contact with the restaurant, saying that he felt "like trying to work outside" after attending a motivation course held by Samhall's personal development team. The restaurant needed extra personnel for a few weeks to cater for Christmas buffets, and he was offered a job assisting in the kitchen with "washing-up, cleaning and miscellaneous tasks," as the representative for the restaurant put it, pointing out: "There is a lot to do now, before Christmas." The Samhall supervisor agreed with the head of the restaurant that Samhall would pay the wage, as he had already done for earlier practice periods involving personnel from Samhall.

In those cases, while the aim of the practice was preparation for a transition, it also concerned establishing contacts with a potential employer, as well giving an opportunity for the employer and Samhall to get an idea of how the employee would function in the specific work environment before entering into an agreement about a transition. However, according to staff member with responsibility for the transition work for several Samhall units who also arranged training posts, most of the periods of practice culminated in the employee returning to Samhall when Samhall's subsidy ran out. He believed that this was because the practice had been a "reality shock" for the employee:

> It turns out that most of them can't tackle the stress. When you have been out doing your practice, you often quit. Things become messy, too muddled. It's a shock for the employee. I usually say to the employer that many of our employees have had a tough time and that they are a little fragile. If this is understood during the initial reception ... you can get a really great employee. They are fragile, so they need a gentle kind of introduction.

One supervisor said that occupationally disabled employees seldom want to leave the external job, but instead, as soon as the "free month is over for the employer, it's thanks and goodbye," and one manager at a work place where Samhall had trainees emphasized: "Without allowances, we would never be able to accept these people here."

All practice periods should be further evaluated by the employee's supervisor gathering impressions about the employee from the instructor at the external work place. "They may have seen things that we missed," one supervisor explained, and another supervisor pointed out: "They live in another world, and can see our employees through other eyes, as it were." The evaluation of the period of practice is documented on a form, "Evaluation of Practice," which is signed by the employee and the manager of the external work place. The original is kept at the Samhall work place and filed in the employee's case file along with the other documents about the person in question.

For this reason, one supervisor thought that it was important that occupationally disabled employees at trainee work places were open about the problems that had led to their placement at Samhall: "Now all cards have to be put on the table. The employer should know what kind of person this is, otherwise problems can easily occur." Another supervisor observed:

> In the presence of their colleagues [at the trainee work place], I don't think they are all that happy about saying what things are like. There may be someone who has a painful back but who is actually a alcoholic. But it is important to be honest so that there are no question marks.

An administrative official at the NEO explained that in order for the practice to work, the "existing personnel must be very well prepared" by being given information about the problems of the occupationally disabled employee, with the aim that the Samhall employee should be "accepted as a fellow worker, and so that it is some kind of dignified work."

Returns

While the periods of practice do not always result in transitions, transitions themselves are not always permanent. One document emphasizes that all occupationally disabled employees leaving Samhall through transitions:

> have the right to return to Samhall up to a period of 12 months (so-called "return"). This "right to re-employment" was introduced in 1983 to make it easier for people to dare to take the step of trying other jobs on the regular labor market. This possibility is important, especially for the employee, who would otherwise never dare to give it a try.

Returns to Samhall are seldom mentioned in Samhall's information material except in the annual reports. There is no information about returns in the newly published advertising brochure *Samhall: More than Just a Job* (which is also available in English) or in an advertising supplement enclosed with a leading Swedish newspaper, where instead it is mentioned that between 1,200 and 1,500 employees leave Samhall each year "for jobs with other employers." For instance, according to the Annual Report for 2003, the number of transitions in 2002 amounted to 973, which corresponded to 4.3 percent of the total workforce of occupationally disabled employees. The number of returns during 2002 and 2003 was reported as 36 percent, but the right to return covers a period of 12 months, so a final report of the number of returns during 2003 could only be made in the accounts for the 2004 financial year. Thus, the figure of 36 percent does not reflect to the final total. However, the Annual Report did not provide any final account of the number of returns for 2001 and 2002, which the 2002 Annual Report had provisionally indicated as 33 percent. Samhall's internal statistics about returns specified that 23 percent of the returns were a result of the employer not extending employment, 49 percent because the activity was terminated or due to lack of work, 10 percent because the employee was not satisfied, and the other 18 percent for other unspecified reasons. The most recent government study about Samhall stated that the return rate during the 1980s was around 20 percent, during the 1990s around 40 percent, and had fallen to approximately 35 percent during recent years. Naturally, it is in the interest of Samhall and the NEO to bring about transitions, which "shows that they have successfully carried out their assignment," as one of the occupationally disabled employees said. However, Samhall's target fulfillment is assessed on gross transitions, not net transitions, and returns in this context do not constitute a formal failure.

Some of the occupationally disabled employees thought that some employers exploited the wage allowance to secure inexpensive staff for the period of a year. Several persons reported that when the first year came to an end, many were terminated and had to return to Samhall, despite being happy with the job and wanting to stay. An NEO administrative official observed that employers tended to back out after the first year, "unless they have been guaranteed wage support for several years ahead." In that respect, returns can be predicted. For this reason, a CD-ROM for supervisors distributed by Samhall stated: "A work place [at Samhall] must be able to receive a 'return' at short notice. Good contacts between Samhall and the new work place guarantee a planned return. Many returns can be predicted."

In general, one supervisor did not believe that exploitation of the wage allowance system took place, even if "undoubtedly there are a few rotten eggs." One of his colleagues said: "In many small communities, this would look very bad." An NEO administrative official declared: "There is always a risk of abuse … and we can only go as far as to see if the company has sufficient insurance and does not owe taxes. In other words, most work well." An information CD-ROM distributed by Samhall states: "Samhall's ambition is that serious employers will recruit personnel from Samhall." An administrative official at the NEO declared: "One should be aware that we are talking about a mutual utilization. The employee has the opportunity of working instead of being sick-listed or similar, and of testing his or her ability. And the employer receives an contribution towards his business."

Some supervisors at Samhall and administrative officials at the NEO were of the opinion that it was the occupationally disabled employees rather than the employers that caused returns: "It can be really stressful out there," declared one supervisor. A supervisor who only worked on arranging transitions at the request of several Samhall units believed that the returns stemmed from the fact that the occupationally disabled employees were not happy: "You become isolated at the new work place. You are different. Perhaps you find that you can't manage the job so well. I also think that they feel that others know that they are receiving allowances, that they are not like the others." He also believed that the insecurity in the new employment compared to the Samhall position with regard to the risk for notice of termination could play a role: "Often they ask, 'What if the company were to become bankrupt a year from now?' I believe one has a great need for security when one has a disability."

An administrative official at the NEO with long experience of transition from Samhall to other employers thought that returns took place because:

> There is too great a difference between outside and inside Samhall. People can often be unprepared for what it can be like to work outside. They have become used to a specific environment, and sometimes there is quite a large difference between the environment at Samhall and the corresponding environment at another company – not only with regard to production requirements, but also other, social requirements, all kinds of things you can take into account in the working situation. People don't look at you in the same way at a work place outside Samhall.

One supervisor believed that the most common reason for an employer not wanting to retain a Samhall employee was that the person was often "sick and didn't come to work, perhaps might come in for a week and then stay at home the following week without saying anything. There are demands on them that they should be present," thus an NEO official felt that returns "are more likely to depend on the employee" than the employer.

Chapter 14
Lock-in as Disabled

Despite Samhall's goal that all clients should eventually leave the organization for a job in the regular labor market, most of them remain at Samhall. As mentioned earlier, supervisors believed that transitions were difficult to realize because the employees did not want to exit Samhall. One supervisor said: "As soon as I submit a suggestion for a job [outside Samhall], they answer that that wasn't what they were thinking about, too far to travel and so on." Another supervisor thought:

> The occupationally disabled don't want to. They are uncertain, many are afraid, many have perhaps been out and become laid off and consequently lost their self-confidence. When they go outside Samhall, they are confronted by uncertainty. They may be afraid, be terminated. The company may close down. You often hear them asking, 'What shall we do if they close down?', and they are right to do so. ... I believe they feel assurance at Samhall, great assurance, plus they have so many they know here, a feeling of fellowship, the social aspect. You are not left out here.

Another supervisor observed:

> During the personal development discussions, most people say, "I am so happy. Everything's great. I have really good friends," and if things are so satisfactory, then we shouldn't do so much. They just don't want to do anything else. Plus they know that perhaps they wouldn't have been able to do anything else ... outside Samhall. This is their life, their world, these are their friends.

A government study concluded, after having interviewed a number occupationally disabled employees: "The interviewed occupationally disabled declared that they felt a strong social security in the relationship they have developed with fellow workers and management personnel at Samhall. The occupationally disabled conveyed the impression that it was difficult to imagine finding similar security elsewhere."

An administrative official at the NEO was of the opinion that "Many people within Samhall have real fellowship. They meet at weekends and in the evenings, and they can be difficult to get out onto the open labor market." A colleague of his commented that at a work place at Samhall, the employees were "really difficult to get out anyway, for they were so terribly happy at work." A government study found:

A factor reported to give positive motivation and driving force is the "we-feeling" that people more or less strongly feel they experience within the Samhall companies that were examined. A factor that contributes to that we-feeling is that people assembled round a common value-system that occurred as an effect of working at Samhall and not out "on the open market." In this case, "we" are the Samhall employees, "they" are the people outside.

For this reason, one manager of a Samhall work place believed: "Many people feel, 'I see, you want to get rid of us in order to achieve your goals [with transition], you want us out just so you will look successful.' That's the way many react." An administrative official at the NEO believed that many Samhall employees thought:

Why should I venture out into uncertainty and the cold? Samhall says that they can't fire us due to the lack of work … and if you come from another country and all that that involves in the form of terror experiences, then you don't want to move. Then there are many other groups with intellectual disabilities that have tried jobs on the open labor market but that have been treated badly. You feel secure there [at Samhall]. You have your friends there. Security is preferred to development. If you are badly treated, the primary thing is not to develop and be like everyone else. The primary thing is, "I'm not treated badly here."

Samhall: The Only Option?

Samhall's CEO believed: "For our employees, Samhall has become their backbone in life. Many of our employees were previously excluded, not only from working life, but even from social life, and this means that one doesn't have the security outside of the job that we [the non-occupationally disabled] have." One supervisor declared, "Our employees often lack social contacts. They are lonely," and that a job at Samhall was therefore a way of "improving social life." Another supervisor felt: "Many have been unemployed for several years. They have perhaps failed all their lives, they have been excluded at many companies. There hasn't been a place for them on the team. Many have poor self-confidence."

A colleague at another work place pointed out:

For many people here, it is the only thing they have and there is an immense difference compared to other companies. They have no social network at home, they have no family or children. When they come home, they sit down and watch TV. Work is then very important, for they have their friends and acquaintances here.

Thus, according to a supervisor: "The unique thing with Samhall is that there is a job for the disabled. They feel there is meaning in going to a work place. I believe that the social bit means a lot to them, they have fellowship." The then

CEO concluded in a document about Samhall: "For anyone with a disability living isolated in his or her home, social fellowship is even more important than for the non-disabled who have more ... options in life."

These ideas are variations on the theme of the occupationally disabled as helpless, exploited and dependent as a result of their personal conditions in the form of poor health, social problems and so on. For example, a report from Statistics Sweden indicated that the functionally disabled were often lonely people without normal social contacts in the form of relations, neighbors and friends. A government study pointed out that people with functional disorders are especially exposed and helpless, and that the demands made on most people to use their own initiative or to obtain information are impossible for many functionally disabled people. One government study observed: "The work with transitions is rendered more difficult by the fact that the occupationally disabled lack sufficient incentives to leave Samhall. For many occupationally disabled employees, security of employment is valuable." Based on an interview study, it also concluded:

> In the first place, the majority of the interviewed occupationally disabled imply that they value the fact that their job at Samhall is secure. In many cases it is about people who, prior to employment at Samhall, had been in work for many years but who had been laid off due to lack of work or illness, and because of this had been unemployed for a longer period. Normally, the work rate is lower at Samhall and the company has substantial job security.

Another study concluded: "The picture of the occupationally disabled as being poorly motivated to leave is confirmed in the interviews carried out in the group of occupationally disabled. Only one of those interviewed indicates that he/she was interested in a job outside of Samhall." A person working on transitions and training posts at Samhall was of the opinion that when there were problems before and after a practice or transition, this was because, "We have not succeeded in motivating our employees. You have to show how positive it will be for the employees to leave." In that respect, a supervisor said, "Often people are not motivated to leave. They are afraid," and one of her colleagues explained: "If you bring up the issue of practice, they stay at home for a week."

A Harsh External World?

According to supervisors, one important reason for difficulties with transitions was a harsh labor market in general, and a hopeless work market for the occupationally disabled in particular, for whom continued employment at Samhall seems to be the only realistic alternative. A government study in 1997 established:

> The supervisors point out two partial explanations for the problem of bringing about transitions. One partial explanation exists externally, and constitutes the

harsh climate on the labor market. The other partial explanation exists internally, and concerns the fact that the occupationally disabled in general have low motivation or a great resistance to finding their way out onto the open labor market.

One supervisor explained, "A prerequisite for being able to leave for another job is that there is a job to go to," and one of his colleagues observed: "It is impossible to effect transitions as long as the labor market is the way it is."

This opinion is also propagated repeatedly within Samhall through the staff magazine, information videos and discussion themes at work place meetings directed at the occupationally disabled employees. A Samhall brochure available at Samhall work places states: "Unemployment is higher among people with functional disorders than among others. Therefore, Samhall plays an important role on the current and future labor market." In a magazine article, Samhall's CEO wrote:

> The current labor market is characterized by structural changes and closures. At the same time, the demands for competence and flexibility are increasing. Long-term sick-listings and disability pensions are on the increase. This development clearly shows that in the foreseeable future there will be a need for a number of different labor market efforts to safeguard the possibilities for work for the functionally disabled with several exposed groups in working life. I am convinced that Samhall will play an important role as one of these efforts.

Hence, to the extent that one defines oneself as occupationally disabled, the message is clear: the labor market *is* more or less hopeless.

In their interviews with the occupationally disabled people, the authors of a government study found that "The occupationally disabled express resignation at the thought of obtaining and coping with a job outside of Samhall," which was based on the notion that their injuries, disabilities and other problems created limitations for them on the open labor market. One of the employees who was interviewed felt, "I wouldn't be able to cope with a job out there," and another said: "There are no jobs to get. It feels meaningless to try." One of the younger employees who had previously worked in a food store was convinced after six years at Samhall that working in food stores was not for him any longer: "The job is too much – too much responsibility," he stated, "I need peace and quiet, otherwise I feel bad."

Several occupationally disabled employees at Samhall felt that they needed to work under the sheltered conditions offered by Samhall. One of them explained: "It's harder out there [at external work places], but on the other hand, they are healthy. Samhall is calmer and more secure." A colleague of his thought that it is was important to "work at one's own pace," and another employee explained: "Here things are adapted to my capability. That's good, because my body is the worse for wear." Another occupationally disabled employee said that it was important not to have to work in a "hectic and stressful environment, for I can't cope with that, then I feel bad, and that's why I am here." A woman explained that previously she had worked in a food store, and there, "I sustained repetitive strain injuries." At Samhall, where she worked on filing activities, she thought: "The stress isn't as apparent as in normal work places." A colleague of hers said: "You are able to work. You don't have to stress. At a normal company, you have to be healthy to keep up," and a person at another work place thought: "You can't demand that sick people should work so quickly."

One of the employees, an immigrant from former Yugoslavia who was a graduate engineer but who worked as a cleaner at Samhall, said in a radio report that personally, he had to take responsibility and "fight," and that he used to be "best" – best at university, best in his previous jobs, and best cleaner at Samhall: "I have thought a lot about leaving Samhall, of finding something for a normal person, but unfortunately I can't count on finding something tomorrow." Two former miners who had come to Samhall when their mines closed did not see any alternative to Samhall, especially in and around the community in which they lived: "What can you do when there is only Samhall for people like me, old and worn out?", one of them asked. An immigrant, a woman of around 50 years of age who spoke poor Swedish and who worked at a Samhall work place in which there were other women in the same age bracket and from the same language area, saw few opportunities for work outside Samhall due to "injuries, age, language."

An employee at another Samhall work place believed: "Because of the state of the labor market, the only chance for me is to work here. I have no chance anywhere else. The National Employment Office has also informed me of this." A middle-aged man asked: "What chances are there for jobs outside when even young people can't get jobs?" One of the occupationally disabled employees pointed out the special needs that he had as a sick and disabled person, "In comparison with other work places, the benefit here is that I can take my problems into consideration," and another of the employees thought that he could imagine working outside of Samhall, but only providing he could obtain a wage allowance so that "I can be at home a few days when I don't feel that well, or work at a more steady pace if I need to."

As mentioned earlier, most occupationally disabled employees said that Samhall was not something they had chosen voluntarily or as their first option, which also added to the feeling that Samhall was the only alternative for them on the labor market. "This is the last outpost," as one occupationally disabled employee observed. One person confined to a wheelchair due to multiple sclerosis was a trained doctor with additional specialist training, and worked at assembling painters' rollers. He said: "I came to Samhall. I had no alternative. I couldn't work as a doctor. I had too much pain. I didn't want to sacrifice my health." He emphasized: "The job is very important, otherwise I would feel worthless and isolated. It's good to get out during the day and have different activities." A man working in one of Samhall's mechanical workshops said: "I came here for the lack of anything else, and things have not improved out there with regard to jobs since that time." One woman explained: "Samhall is not something you choose. You finally end up here. You are transferred here by the National Employment Office."

In an interview in a government study, one supervisor said that he wanted to protect his employees from the harsher demands in the open labor market: "The tougher the climate is out there, the more our employees are excluded in here. I feel greatly on their behalf, and I disassociate myself from a society that allows exclusion in this way." Another supervisor observed, "Conditions are not easy for many disabled at other work places. They are often victimized," and one of the employees declared that it was great working at Samhall to avoid feeling alienated in society, since: "You are judged if you have a disability." In that respect, a supervisor explained that Samhall "has a much larger safety net – take, for example, the problem with drugs. On the open labor market, you don't get many chances before you are fired, but here at Samhall there are people who only work on supporting and helping such people." He gave the example of one of the employees who was "gravely alcoholic" and who "should not remain there according to the law," but: "It wouldn't feel good to send him away. We know what happens. He will fall through the safety net. We turn a blind eye to his being here."

Keeping the Disabled

Some supervisors believed that another reason for the problems in realizing transitions could be found in demands for the maintenance of good, businesslike production. One Samhall document establishes: "The transitions involve the employees who have experience and are trained in the job leaving Samhall and being replaced by new employees, who, because of their occupational disability, can have considerable difficulties and comprehensive needs for on-job training." For that reason, it is "mostly the middle layer that will have to go, not key people," one supervisor explained. Another supervisor pointed out that for many years the state paid 170 percent compensation for additional costs – 100 percent wage cover and 70 percent disability adaptation – but that the current compensation for costs was only 70 percent, which "doesn't even cover wages." "There is little wonder that we keep the strongest people in production," he concluded. A colleague of his observed: "The unit has its mainstays, and I try not to pass on these people in the first place, but the middle register who are weaker, primarily so that I can manage myself, so that I don't have to supervise the job, but assist with the job."

An NEO administrative official thought that there was a dilemma for those at Samhall who were "too capable," since "they keep production going." He believed that the most appropriate candidates for a transition were "seldom identified as ready for a transition" by the supervisors. Another administrative official at the NEO observed: "There are people that they [Samhall] need to cope with for production who are very capable and who could very well hold their own on the labor market, as we see it." In an interview in the staff magazine, a supervisor thought: "We supervisors are in breach of our duty if we organize work so that everything depends on certain key people. This would put a brake on transition work."

One supervisor did not feel that there was anyone among his 40 employees who was suitable for a transition: "I have a team that works. My assignments work so well now," he observed. A government study found that there was a tendency among supervisors to keep "the most able and most productive personnel." One person within Samhall who only worked on transitions on behalf of supervisors at different work places said: "One has to recognize the contradiction in Samhall's activities. You are employed to do a good job, and the next minute you have to leave. You are to be parted from the best, although you have responsibility for activities." One of his colleagues working in a corresponding assignment in another part of the country thought: "They have exaggerated the demand for efficiency and profitability. They should have realized that this is not a normal company." A radio report pointed out: "Production at Samhall should be carried out on a businesslike basis, but at the same time the state demands that the company should stimulate employees to seek work out on the open labor market. Having to always to get rid of competence is a problematic goal for a company." This was borne out by a government study, which emphasized:

> If the employee during his or her time at Samhall has gained experience and become skilled and thus obviously contributes toward the economic goals, there is no motive for the local management at Samhall – which also has to comply with economic requirements – to contribute toward a transition to the regular labor market.

Despite the supervisor's formal responsibility for "assessing transition maturity," as one of them put it, the real responsibility for transitions lies with the occupationally disabled people themselves. One supervisor declared that the occupationally disabled employees must "be ready with their process," and that they must arrive at "what they want to do outside Samhall." She explained that during the personal development discussions, she used to ask, "What do you want to do after Samhall?", but also emphasized that "You [the employee] have to give me the assignment. You are the one who should know what you want and which companies you would like me to contact." At a meeting with around forty employees, another supervisor said, "I promise that I will never force you to do anything, for example transitions. The initiative must come from you," which is in line with the perception in an information CD for supervisors at Samhall: "There are no simple short cuts to successful transitions. Fundamental is respect for the fact that each employee plays 'the starring role in his or her own life' and supporting the person to take personal responsibility for their own development."

In a report in a magazine, "Those who are always left," about a number of Samhall employees at one of Samhall's packaging workshops, one of the employees, a 34-year-old woman who had worked at Samhall for seven years, said: "I don't want to be here all my life. I feel terrible here!" A passage read: "Ellinore has a lump in her throat. She works at picking up screws, counting then in the palm of her hand and then placing them back in the red plastic box again." She continued:

> You can't get anywhere. No new challenges, just the same things day and day out. Sometimes I feel as if I am nothing! For example, it would be wonderful to work at a daycare center – lovely to get away from this. ... At the same time, I am afraid of not having anything to do. Just sitting at home would break me.

At a work place with approximately fifty employees, one of the employees said: "Some of us must go on, and want to leave this place. There are seven of us who have decided that we have to get out, but hush! Don't say anything!" In one group of occupationally disabled workers, there was talk about leaving the company and various ideas for leaving were discussed, such as getting together and starting a business. The supervisor at the work place in question, who was very aware of the wishes of the employees, commented on it all: "Many of them want to do so much, but they can't." Supervisors seldom worked actively themselves at making contact with external work places. One of them emphasized: "It's up to the personnel to make those contacts." One employee described how he had provided several suggestions of companies that might be interested in accepting him, but "the supervisor said that things weren't just right at the moment." One of the employees pointed out that it might be problematic to make contact with external employers during working hours, as "You have to leave your job and so on, and this isn't always so easy." One employee wrote in a book about Samhall: "If we are going to the National Employment Office or doing something else to seek a job or training, we have to clock out. ... I have not received any help from Samhall to seek any other 'normal' job" (Aulin, 2001).

One supervisor observed that there were "those who wanted to leave. They did everything to leave. But then there were those who wanted to leave, but who didn't have the ability. They haven't understood, they believe they can do it, but I know that they won't be able to." Another supervisor thought:

> Going on year after year after year, plodding away at the same thing, the people who have worked here a long time, I don't think we can get those to leave, that we can pass them on to the open market. They are so terribly secure. They know how things function at Samhall. They are completely destroyed if you talk to them about life outside Samhall. Then there are those who have great self-confidence, who believe that they can cope with most things, which they can't. Then you have to stop that person and teach this first before you continue.

Becoming Locked In as Disabled

One of the employees, a man of around 25, related that when he was new at Samhall, he was optimistic about being able to leave the company soon, "It would only be temporary," but that now, after six years' employment, "I don't care any more." A newly employed occupationally disabled person emphasized: "I want to leave. At least I am not going to stay here all my life." In 2003, another person, who had previously worked as a car mechanic said, "The idea was that I would be here for a year. I have been here since 1985," and a colleague of his who had worked in Samhall for 12 years, declared: "I never thought I would be here so long." One woman related about herself and a colleague: "We have worked at Samhall for 15 and 17 years respectively, and for 15 and 17 years respectively we have wanted to leave." One of the employees at another work place emphasized that it was important not to stay at Samhall too long, for "If you have been here too long, you give up, you lose your initiative." "You shouldn't be here [at Samhall] too long!", one supervisor declared, since "the older employees [become] mother and father figures and take care of the younger employees."

One of the employees pointed out that he believed that "self-confidence" did not improve, but got worse from working at Samhall, because: "They force you to carry out simple, therapeutic jobs so that eventually you believe you can't do anything." Another of the employees said: "If your self-confidence is good, it gets worse here. After a time, you feel worthless," And a third person thought, "You are oppressed here. And then they get the idea that you will have to leave when you have been floored. If you aren't crazy when you begin here, you'll become crazy eventually." Yet another employee said: "First you are broken, and then you lose your power of initiative, and then you get to hear that you yourself have the solution to your problem." Thus, several occupationally disabled workers were generally disappointed that "Samhall has not managed to arrange a job for me," as one of them put it, or that "Samhall doesn't take any responsibility for me," as another said.

At a workshop, one young man maintained: "It's important not to stay too long here, for then you easily become permanent." He thought that the job was monotonous and "you are tied to certain assignments. Eventually, you become fixed in your mind." An administrative official at the NEO reported that many of the younger new employees at Samhall had a strong belief in their own ability, "So there, you almost have to apply the brakes, for they don't know their capabilities." The official observed that the younger people she had recruited to Samhall over the years still worked there, which she believed was due to "security, and if you work with these kind of monotonous assignments, you automatically get stuck, you lose faith in learning anything new. Finally, you don't believe in your own ability." A woman of around 60 who had worked at Samhall for twenty years thought that the company must "go in for getting the young to leave. We older people are a lost cause. Many young people establish roots easily. It's easy to remain at Samhall," and a colleague of hers explained: "When I was new here, I believed that I would soon leave. I was active and applied for other jobs, had plans, but after a while I gave up." Several younger men at one of Samhall's work places observed that when they began at Samhall, they "heard several times that Samhall was only something temporary, a step along the way," as one of them declared. One supervisor thought: "Most people who have been at Samhall for more than three to four years are very difficult to get out. Transition should happen during the first year."

One government study recently found:

> Today, of Samhall's employees with an occupational disability, almost 40 percent have been employed in the company for more than ten years. After this long period at Samhall, most of them have come to regard their employment at Samhall as a secure position. The longer employment at Samhall lasts, the less the possibility of leaving Samhall.

Under the heading "Locking-in Effects," another government study of Samhall stated: "People with a long period of employment [at Samhall] are less likely to go over to a job on the regular labor market." A nurse at Samhall's corporate health service believed: "We have many who have worked here for many years, and they have become adapted to Samhall and find it difficult to imagine anything else." An NEO administrative official who had worked with transitions of Samhall employees for several years explained: "They've stopped thinking about normal jobs in the future."

However, in several publications, Samhall has reported examples of people who have left Samhall. In an advertising supplement in a leading Swedish newspaper, there was a story about a man who had been placed at Samhall fifteen years earlier after being sick-listed for three years because of an occupational injury, but who had obtained a one-year temporary appointment with a local authority a year before the interview. He concluded: "Thanks to Samhall, I am now back in normal working life again." In one of the annual reports, there was a story about a man who had left Samhall after twenty years of employment:

> After personal development efforts and support from labor management, Leif Åslund at Samhall in Karlstad found his dream job: at the Pärlan Restaurant.
> – "I would never have dared take the step over to this job if I hadn't completed the Samhall course 'Dare to Win.'" This was the start of something new for Leif.
> – "Above all, during recent years I have dared to do more things thanks to the opportunities I have received through Samhall."

The transition for Leif was such a success that he "has now exchanged his part-time pension [which he subsequently received during his employment at Samhall] for full-time work at the restaurant" – all of a sudden, he became less occupationally disabled when he left Samhall.

One supervisor interviewed for a government study believed that development and rehabilitation should not be Samhall's official goal for large groups of the occupationally disabled:

> Many of those working here are too old to have any chance on the labor market. If you are over the age of 50, lack education and have several functional disorders, you don't have a chance on today's labor market. What is activation for them? No, our task is a different one. We must ensure that they have a tolerable existence for the rest of their working life.

The same study reported that supervisors did not feel that it was possible to achieve any personal development aimed at rehabilitating the employee to work outside Samhall:

> The supervisors declare that once people have got a job at Samhall, they tend to remain within the company and in most of the cases, Samhall feels that there is justification for keeping the occupationally disabled in the company. One assumes that the reason for this is that the majority of the occupationally disabled have such far-reaching functional disorders that employment on the open labor market under prevailing circumstances is impossible. ... The supervisors also state those who would probably be able to cope with employment outside Samhall lack the motivation or/and self-confidence to leave.

The fact that Samhall's employees do a solid job helping the elite of Swedish companies deliver products all over the world, and the way in which they contribute toward Samhall's production of high-quality services and goods that are in demand with customers in both Sweden and abroad, seems to have little bearing on other employers considering individual employees employable. Some of the employees pointed out that their attractiveness on the open labor market had been weakened by their position at Samhall due to the stigma of being employed as an occupationally disabled worker: "Nobody regarded me as occupationally disabled before I began at Samhall," one of them declared. One of the employees wrote in a book about Samhall (Aulin, 2001) that Samhall should change its name, as "The name is often associated with those that work there, that is, the physically and mentally disabled. Because of the name, there is a rumor that we are 'feeble-minded'! This is not correct!" Another employee said that he was convinced that "people in town" thought, "'There are only idiots there [at Samhall]," and a colleague of his thought: "They [Samhall] say that it is a springboard, but when you mention Samhall, then it's all over," in terms of contacts with external employers. One of the occupationally disabled employees believed that she could understand employers being skeptical about employing personnel from Samhall: "A position at Samhall implies that you have a problem, so it is only logical that they [as employers] think, 'Will he stay at home and be sick a lot?'" As a result, one of her colleagues believed: "It's difficult to say that you have worked at

Samhall when applying for other jobs." In a magazine report about Samhall staff at one of Samhall's work places, one of the employees declared: "You can hardly get another job after working here. Nobody wants you when you have worked at Samhall."

Chapter 15
Good Intentions, Misunderstood Results?

Despite the general emphasis on the significance of offering Samhall employees activating work for the occupationally disabled and the official statements that the work is meaningful and developing, one supervisor declared: "I have people here with a university education that sit packing nails into plastic bags. I can think of it sometimes, but most often I dismiss it because it becomes too troubling." One problem in this context, as one of his colleagues pointed out, is that "Samhall's jobs are intended for the weakest people," but that "even the strongest people have to perform these." He described a department at one work place where a group of occupationally disabled employees sat assembling painters' rollers, which entailed taking the roller holders from a carton, installing the rollers, then placing the finished product in another carton: "The work is perfect for several people in group, but for others is just too simple," the supervisor observed. A salesman at Samhall said:

> What I have experienced many times over all these years is (1) we don't believe that our employees can do as much as they can, (2) that we demand too little of our employees. We have a huge differentiation when it comes to the work capacity of our employees compared to that of a normal company, and thus we must be good at making demands on those that *can* produce a lot, *can* do a lot theoretically, but we have been a little stupid in that respect. We start with the lowest common denominator for our employees.

A member of corporate management pointed out: "One shouldn't underestimate the ability of our employees. Many times *we* place limiting factors on them by deciding how things are." Another Samhall manager stated: "Many are actually quite good at working." In this context, an occupationally disabled employee claimed, "There is a lot of prejudice about us among the supervisors," and another explained:

> Many times I have said to the boss, "I would be able to do that and that too," but each time I've had to hear, "You wouldn't be able to do that. It demands speed," or "This is probably not for you. You have to be able to tolerate stress to do that."

One manager at Samhall noted in the staff magazine that there was "a lot of prejudice about Samhall's personnel, and great ignorance about what our employees are able to tackle successfully."

Supervisors sometimes felt that they had been "positively surprised" by the occupationally disabled, as one of them put it. One manager said: "It's turned out that even people with an occupational disability can make an activity economically viable." Another supervisor observed: "Sometimes the occupationally disabled are shrewd themselves. Some of them are technical. They learn on their own," and a member of corporate management remembered that he had been surprised when an occupationally disabled employee had managed to carry out a fair number of technically complicated activities successfully. One supervisor pointed out that many supervisors he had met "do not believe in the personnel, but they [the personnel] know more than you think. Many of them actually have good solutions and ideas, but often they don't dare take them up themselves."

The occupationally disabled employees did not always feel that Samhall provided the basis for development and learning that it is often said to offer. In a book about Samhall, one of the occupationally disabled employees wrote about the growing practice of hiring Samhall personnel to other companies: "People who are hired out to other companies from Samhall are given the lousy jobs." One of his colleagues said, "I want to work at a normal work place again. I want to be treated like all the rest," and another declared: "They say 'meaningful and developing work.' But sitting gluing paper days on end – do you think that is developing? All we hear is that we should develop, but that doesn't happen." Another employee who packaged toys for a few hours each morning but usually didn't have any work to do in the afternoon observed: "This is therapeutic work, but time drags nevertheless." A co-worker of his believed: "This is not activation for me, but more a way of having a job." An employee at another work place said: "There's no development here, just work." A man at a workshop observed: "It's no fun sitting installing rollers, but what can I do? I'm a workaholic, I can't just sit at home." Another employee declared, "The job is so goddamn monotonous. The only time you can get away from it is when you're sick," and a colleague of his wrote in a book about Samhall: "I've worked for 13 years at a Samhall workshop. The assignments we carry out here are monotonous." A colleague of his said, "At Samhall they are always talking about developing. What does 'to develop' mean? Development implies that you keep getting new and more difficult assignments. It's not like that here." A woman working in a large-scale kitchen reported: "They say that Samhall is for rehabilitation. But you don't get better here. I have never been rehabilitated, and I've worked at Samhall for 15 years now."

One supervisor observed that many of his employees were dissatisfied with their employment at Samhall, "Naturally, people feel that it isn't developing to go picking up things for days on end. They lose faith in the system," pointing out that there was a "problem with confidence" at Samhall: "There is a lack of trust. The occupationally disabled do not trust us, and we [supervisors] do not trust them." Talking about development, learning, change and other positively charged terms only creates cynicism and a general feeling of resignation among some of the occupationally disabled when the target group's experience is that this is not always realized: "Personal development discussions, that's just a load of crap," one of the employees declared. Another of them believed that it would "be better not to be hypocritical," but instead, "Tell us like it is – that this is a dead end."

The most recent government study of Samhall concluded: "It is not enough merely to provide work for people with occupational disabilities. Even people with occupational disabilities have a right to demand both meaningful employment and a job that is developing." The fact that many at Samhall incur occupational injuries or are sick-listed during their employment at Samhall adds to a perception that people do not become more employable through their Samhall career. One employee related that earlier in her professional career she had seldom been on the sick list, but since coming to Samhall, she "often felt bad and was home a lot." Another employee wrote in a contribution to a book about Samhall (Aulin, 2001), "I have more pain now than I had when I began [at Samhall]," and a relative of a Samhall employee wrote in the same book that Samhall recruited "completely healthy people" who "have to work themselves to the bone in a mass of meaningless monotonous jobs which the open market automated a long time ago. My relative has pains in his arms and shoulders since he came to Samhall. They weren't there before." One of the employees observed in the same book that "many become passive" by working at Samhall.

Several of the occupationally disabled employees were of the opinion that their own suggestions and initiatives in daily working life were seldom encouraged. In a book, one of them felt that "If you come with your own ideas, these are quickly brushed aside," and another employee wrote: "We feel like robots, and not like people when we work." Yet another employee wrote in his contribution: "After so many years within the company, I've learned exactly how the ideal Samhall worker should be constituted: you shouldn't object, not think at all, accept everything corporate management devises, and even be glad and thankful for the great honor of working there."

In the same book, another Samhall employee wrote: "My belief when I began there [was] that this should be rehabilitation, but if anything, the opposite was true. Many don't feel well, but unfortunately, too few dare to say anything. The fear of reprisals from corporate management is great, which I have personally experienced through relocation." Another employee wrote that Samhall had:

> become a territorial-minded colossus that has outlived its day, in my mind primarily because of incompetent directly employed individuals in leading positions who are so jealous of their meal ticket that they kick at everything and everyone, including those who exhibit good judgment, civil courage, and to top that, personal initiative!

Another employee wrote: "Beginning work at Samhall results in complete loss of one's human dignity. At this work place, the occupationally disabled employees are subjected to various kinds of abuse by the so-called labor management if they exhibit the least suspicion of personal initiative or individual thought."

One occupationally disabled person said that during lunchtime, he used to draw aside to work on private things, "to keep my brain working," and showed a little room where he was busy building model aircraft and cars from drawings he had downloaded from the Internet. This was his "safety zone," as he called it: "Here, I can get away from my colleagues and managers." One of the employees said that when he was new, "I thought a lot about the question of mental retardation and Samhall," and "thought about what this kind of environment could do with me," but "now I only try to switch myself off." In a similar way, several employees at another work place used to solve crosswords during coffee breaks, so that "you don't become a complete block head," as one of them said. One employee who was an immigrant but who had lived in Sweden for around ten years and who worked on packaging thought that Samhall offered "conformist jobs." He pointed out that previously, he had done "interesting project jobs" outside Samhall, that he had studied at university, and that nowadays, after work, "each day I go to the library to read."

One of the employees wrote in a book about Samhall: "The manager claimed that I had criticized the company. I got no help from the union. More likely, they have taken part in the victimization. The union is part of the tragic story of Samhall." Another employee wrote: "It's strange that just because the state is the owner, this treatment can continue, and also with the acceptance of the union." Several Samhall documents emphasize the importance of the company having good relations with labor organizations, and that the union at Samhall has always had a significant rule. One document directed at Samhall supervisors maintained, "The labor organizations have a set role in the daily work on all levels in the Samhall Group. A well-functioning labor union movement should always be encouraged, since it is a good support not only for employees, but even for management and their activities," and emphasized that at individual work places, the union:

> often has great significance for how the work place and labor organization will be developed. The union is also an invaluable asset for managers in various types of organizational changes, and necessary to enable an adjustment process [that is, movement of personnel]. If the manager has good cooperation with the local union branch, this is a powerful support.

Among other things, the work of the union at Samhall is carried out, according to Swedish law, by representatives on the board of directors of Samhall, as well as in the so-called Works Council that Samhall has established, which is a forum for collaboration between Samhall and the labor unions.

To the extent that criticism has been expressed by supervisors and other leading officials at Samhall, it has come from former employees. For example, one former public relations officer wrote in a book: "My own reflection is that generally speaking, the first impression of Samhall is very positive among all those who come into contact with the enterprise. Criticism of the enterprise comes with increased knowledge about the reality that hides behind the facade" (Rådahl, 1990: 17). Another former public relations official at Samhall wrote in a magazine:

> Already after a few months I began to ponder what I was actually doing. I was out and about in the country meeting many people, both on the shop floor and at the director level. I began to acquire impressions. I was really shaken up. Basically, walking around work premises built for so-called sick or disabled people is an abnormal experience.

This kind of criticism from former supervisors has not been common in the general debate about the company (it should be noted that it comes from former public relations officials whose work involved promoting the company's activities to the surrounding world).

Regardless of the character of the criticism, Samhall representatives have felt that the company is misunderstood, which may explain the relatively large number of articles justifying the existence of the company, research studies initiated by the company confirming the viability of the enterprise, marketing campaigns in newspapers and on TV and so on. In a document directed toward molders of public opinion and leading officials in the community who had criticized Samhall, Samhall's CEO explained:

> Then I ask them, "If you had a child or a grandchild who was functionally disordered, do you think they should be at home or in an institution? Would it be good for them?" That's what I usually say, and then most people usually mellow a little. You have no way of knowing if you will have a grandchild or a child tomorrow with a functional disorder requiring an adapted job. And then I can see that someone in the vicinity who has a relative who is functionally disabled understands this much better.

A member of Samhall's corporate management who was also director of communications and had been employed by the company since its formation wrote in Samhall's staff magazine: "Unfortunately, many reports over recent years have been dominated by closures [within Samhall]. If the media reports nothing but closures, all parties concerned will feel quite depressed." In another comment to an external critic of Samhall, the director of communications wrote with regard to a positive editorial in a leading Swedish newspaper: "Perhaps things are finally beginning to swing in our direction?" The director of communications believed that reporting by the media had often been "about distrust and criticism," but that this article constituted an exception: "This was a few minutes' blessed reading for all of us who have fought so long at Samhall. Finally, a journalist who spoke out on behalf of Samhall! Finally, someone who has understood!"

Chapter 16

The Disabling State of an Active Society

In the traditional welfare state, populations were generally divided into workers and various groups of non-workers (see Butcher, 2002; Considine, 2001; Lindert, 2004). Specifically, "to be fully regarded as a social citizen in the welfare society you need to be regarded as a regular worker. Many of the benefits and privileges associated with the welfare state are contingent upon this status" (Walters, 1997: 222). This is a role that has been difficult to bear for a number of disadvantaged groups, most notably disabled people (Drake, 1999; Kvist, 2002). As a result, they have often been relegated to secondary status as social citizens, commonly resulting in inactivity and social exclusion (see, for example, Abberley, 2002; Branson and Miller, 2002). However, this problem has not been limited to them alone. Indeed, one of the main responses to social exclusion in terms of mass unemployment by welfare states has been to reduce the size of the active workforce through, for example, early retirement or disability pensions. A common consequence in many countries has been the permanent exclusion of large groups of citizens from the regular labor market (Bauman, 2007; Goul Andersen et al., 2005).

This policy has become the subject of growing intense criticism, both from neo-liberals and neo-social democrats. First of all, there is the problem of future labor supply (see, for example, Saunders, 2005; Serrano Pascual, 2007; Williams, 1999). If large groups of people are constantly excluded for various moral and social reasons regarding their lack of fitness, the active workforce is likely to shrink, given the generally low birth rates in industrialized countries. Demographic facts argue against the traditional welfare model. Second, there is the fiscal problem. Large groups of people who live on social welfare (perhaps all their lives, which is the case with many disabled people; see, for example, Oorschot and Hvinden, 2001; Lindert, 2004) do not contribute economically to society's progress; from an economic point of view, they are a "burden." In the face of harsh global competition, nations need to constantly reduce their spending in order to stay competitive. Third, the welfare state's division of the populace into "workers" and "non-workers" has led to social unrest and morally disturbing results. Through the unintentional creation of divided societies, some people have become "insiders" while others have become "outsiders" (for example, disabled people). Finally, facing global competition, public and private employers need to become more flexible and entrepreneurial by adopting forms of management that are built around individual subjects' self-governing capabilities and active participation, thus promoting an active and entrepreneurial attitude among *all* existing and prospective employees. In general, critiques of the welfare state have argued that there is both a need to welcome new groups into the labor market, thus recognizing the demand for participation and making employment and activity the norm, and a need to stress the virtues of lifelong learning, employability and change (see Garsten and Jacobsson, 2004).

Based on the present study, it seems plausible to suggest that Samhall is an example of an activation program that, contrary to its intentions, breeds passivity. Despite the idea that Samhall is a central part of the new policy emphasis on activating disabled people through empowerment and rehabilitation, the organization shares features of many traditional disability programs, such as disability pensions and residential or institutional care, in the sense of people becoming progressively locked into a situation of disablement, incapacity and helplessness (see Abberley, 2002; Drake, 1999). Contrary to the new activating regime, however, the old regime did not aim to empower the target group. In the new regime, those who for one reason or another are unable to live up to the norms of being a "normal" and hence fully active citizen are objectified as passive and unemployable people through the same principles that aim to make them active.

Concretely, the realization of this enterprise comes through the work offered at Samhall, which can be regarded as "dirty" in the sense that it stigmatizes those who undertake it. Hughes (1951; 1962) coined the term "dirty work" to describe tasks and occupations that are perceived as disgusting or degrading, and observed that society tends to delegate dirty work to groups who act as agents on society's behalf, and that society then stigmatizes these groups, effectively disowning and disavowing the work it has offered. In Hughes's (1951: 319) terms, dirty work "may be simply physically disgusting. It may be a symbol of degradation, something that wounds one's dignity. Finally, it may be dirty work in that it in some way goes counter to the more heroic of our moral conceptions." Certainly, "dirtiness" is a social construction; it is not something that is inherent in either the work itself or people, but is imputed by people: "Dirty work, after all, does not inhere in a particular task: one occupation's dirty work can be another's sought and fought for prerogative" (Emerson and Pollner, 1975: 244). Or, as Dick (2005: 1368) put it: "Dirt, whether physical or moral, is essentially a matter of perspective, not empirics." Hence, "the common denomination among tainted jobs is not so much their specific attributes but the visceral repugnance of people to them" (Ashforth and Kreiner, 1999: 415). Hughes (1971: 343) stressed that "dirty work of some kind is found in all occupations," and that everyone occasionally has to "play a role of which he thinks he ought to be a little ashamed of morally." People who perform dirty work tend to become stigmatized – indeed, regarded as "dirty" in a sociological sense through society's projection of negative qualities associated with dirt onto them. The perceived taint of the dirty work is projected onto the individuals so that they are seen to personify dirt, thus suggesting a process of "personalization" or "individualization" of some social issue, such as unemployment. Indeed, for a particular society, it is appropriate that some people handle the dirty and distasteful work that is necessary for the functioning of that society, thus enabling the others to continue regarding themselves as clean, and therefore of higher –that is, more "able" and "normal" – standing (see Hughes, 1962: 10). To cite Ashforth and Kreiner (1999: 417):

> The perceived taint of the dirty work is apt to be projected onto the workers so that they are seen to personify dirt. The stigma may be communicated directly through putdowns, reduced deference and respect, and demeaning questions ("How can you do it?") and more subtly through discrimination and avoidance.

This observation has important social implications. As Douglas (2002) noted in her seminal study on cleanliness and order, society tends to draw a sharp distinction between purity and pollution, regarding those who perform dirty work as dirty or polluted themselves. By performing dirty work, people tend to reproduce social norms and ideas about dirty people. By doing dirty work, there is the potential that they *become* dirty through physical, social and moral pollution. As suggested by Ashforth and Kreiner (1999), "physical taint" refers to work that is associated with garbage, waste, bad smells and so on; "social taint" occurs when an occupation involves recurrent contact with people who are themselves regarded as stigmatized, or when the activity being carried out is experienced as degrading, and "moral taint" refers to an occupation of a dubious character, or where the worker employs methods that are deceptive and intrusive. The typical Samhall employee is involved in occupations embodying all taints that can potentially explain the reason why most of them seem to eventually embrace the identity of occupationally disabled.

Of course, it should be noted that the research that has been reported in this book is based on a case study of an activation program in just one country. Still, there may be some useful early insights for the debate about the "active society," particularly taking into account the fact that Sweden's way of addressing activation of the unemployed has similarities to other countries' unemployment policies. Sweden's categorization of unemployed people as disabled in order to direct them toward various activation programs can be seen as the concrete manifestation of the current activation ideology among welfare states, particularly in Europe. Hence, this case may be of interest as a first and exploratory experience, but should be compared with evidence from other countries, where both social and political idiosyncrasies and similarities are spelled out.

Essentially, people suffering from various "impairments" who are recruited by Samhall learn to become disabled by participating in a work organization that is adapted to the presumed needs of disabled people. Hence, occupationally disabled people are reproduced through the activation offered by Samhall. The longer they stay at Samhall, the more disabled they become in a sociological sense – in the sense of acquiring a "disabled self" (see Corker and Shakespeare, 2002; Lane, 1997; Thomas, 2004) – making them all the less likely to leave Samhall. Perhaps an active society, through its emphasis on ability, strength, competence and so on, has raised the bar higher than ever before, therefore an increasing number of people risk "disablement," and indeed end up as "disabled," because they lack the capacity to clear the hurdle (see Bauman, 2007). Potentially, this "sociological disablement" is the result of a modern state's benevolent activities to empower unemployed people by activating them as disabled.

An important implication of the active society is that the individual becomes responsible for his or her predicament, based on the belief that he or she can do something about it: "The active system obliges the active subject to exercise choice, and to undertake an intensive work on the self, as it undertakes to ensure that the social technologies exist to enable work on self to be performed" (Dean, 1995: 581). Or, as Van Berkel et al. (2002: 31) put it, the focus on who is to be blamed has shifted from emphasizing society to emphasizing the unemployed themselves: "This shift has been exacerbated with the emergence of activation policies across Europe, in connection with which not only liberals and conservatives but also labor politicians have increasingly talked about excluded persons' responsibilities for their own lives, and blamed them for their alleged unwillingness to be activated."

Overall, in the Samhall case one can conclude that there is a mismatch between stated goals and ideals and the practical results. Students of social welfare have long acknowledged this phenomenon (see, for example, Goffman, 1961; Gummer, 1990; Resnick and Patti, 1980). Traditional social welfare programs have often been founded on a "restorative approach" to rehabilitation, but they have instead typically pursued an "accommodative approach" in practice (see, for example, Branson and Miller, 2002; Holmqvist, 2008; Lane, 1997; Schram, 2000). A commonsense explanation for this phenomenon is that an activation program such as Samhall's suffers from a number of pathologies regarding its management and overall organization, where responsibility should be laid both on politicians, for their ignorance of some potentially unexpected consequences of these good intentions, and on staff at specific welfare organizations such as Samhall, for their failure to provide a meaningful and enlightening work environment. Given the fact that few people who enter sheltered employment leave for a "regular" job (see Considine, 2001; Lindert, 2004; Wadensjö, 2007), one could argue that the work offered does not necessarily contribute to occupationally disabled employees' activation. To this extent, they are examples of "failures."

Such problems should be relatively easy to address, for example by allocating resources so that greater variation in work content can be proposed at Samhall and in other programs, or by designing policies that emphasize disabled people's capabilities and competencies, rather than their impairments and deficiencies. Another avenue in dealing with these problems would be to design programs where disabled people are able to alternate between jobs at a variety of non-sheltered employers. This would probably allow them to broaden their competency basis significantly, which could contribute to their overall employability so that they could eventually find permanent employment with a "regular" employer. Of course, in such a system care needs to be taken that people are not exploited as cheap, state-subsidized labor, used temporarily during peaks of production.

But perhaps one should rather interpret these programs as "successes," in the sense that they are able to effectively "massage" unemployment statistics, thus illustrating the phenomenon of "hidden unemployment" (Beatty and Fothergill, 2002; Beatty and Fothergill, 2005; De Mooij, 1999; Fieldhouse and Hollywood, 1999). Perhaps the phenomenon under scrutiny here may be explained by harsh *Realpolitik*, or it may simply be seen as an illustration of "organizational hypocrisy," which, among students of organizations, is regarded as a critical way for decision-makers and the organizations they control to adapt to conflicting or even irreconcilable requirements in their environments (see Brunsson, 1989). By "disabling" people, and thus accommodating them in large-scale welfare programs, there is the potential for politicians to "solve" pressing social issues such as unemployment, particularly in regions where there is a weak labor market, concomitant with a form of state-sanctioned provision of inexpensive labor to industry that could contribute to regions' or countries' overall competitiveness. This activity may be an important one, despite sometimes negative consequences for single groups of individuals' welfare and future career prospects. By labeling this enterprise an example of "activation," welfare states' aura as the foremost providers of help to disadvantaged people in a harsh, global and capitalistic world can be retained, and even reinforced.

Following this kind of interpretation, one may also argue that the reason why activation programs disable people is, as explained above, their inherent potential for victim-blaming, whereby active societies stress disabled people's individual responsibilities for their social situation (see, for example, Goul Andersen et al., 2005; Jensen and Pfau-Effinger, 2005; Serrano Pascual, 2007), where responsibility for unsuccessful efforts to find a regular job is shifted to the individual who is seen as sick, impaired and unhealthy (see Conrad and Schneider, 1992; Crawford, 2006). In the active society, people are expected to take responsibility for their health, wellbeing, fitness and competence, irrespective of their physiological or mental status. By claiming that some people are disabled as an explanation for their poor employability, their problems are individualized. The ideology of individualization can promote an idea of "bad living" or "bad behavior" among people that may have important individual and social consequences, such as by acting as a mechanism for deviance amplification by reinforcing the stigma associated with unemployment and disability, in addition to projecting an image of disablement as a personal tragedy rather than as a socially produced state. This critique argues that modern policies for combating social problems that bring the individual's character into focus largely fail to address the consequences of industrial capitalism: social inequalities, poverty, structural discrimination and other social and material disadvantages in people's lives.

Certainly, Sweden and other countries such as Denmark and the Netherlands that are strong proponents of an active approach to unemployment policy and have comprehensive programs for activating the unemployed enjoy among the highest rates of employment. But the number of formally organized disabled people in these countries is also among the highest in Europe (Fujiura and Rutkowski-Kmitta, 2001; Overbye, 2005). Hence, without disabled people, no activation program such as Samhall; without Samhall, no disabled people? As Van Berkel et al. (2002) concluded in their review of inclusion policies in Europe: "Without any exclusion, there would not be any inclusion [policies]: inclusion, so to speak, presupposes the existence of exclusion." It is a familiar observation that "by international comparison, Sweden has an especially strong emphasis on labor market policy programs for the disabled (measured in terms of the proportion of participants or costs)" (Wadensjö, 2007: 131–2). In his study "Dilemmas in Disability Activation and How Scandinavians Try to Live with Them," Overbye (2005: 167) suggested that "high disability prevalence might be the Achilles heel of Scandinavian social policy," suggesting that the great number of excluded disabled people in Scandinavia – despite the many resources devoted to inclusive programs – constitute a failure for society. According to the observations that have been reported here, perhaps it is the other way around – perhaps it is the principal reason why the Scandinavian countries (and particularly Sweden) have become such successful expressions of the active society.

Appendix

I worked in the following Samhall premises on the following tasks that were either located at a contractor's premises or at Samhall's own work places.

Härnösand (Northern Sweden)

One operation was called "distribution of food." Together with eight occupationally disabled Samhall employees who were employed by Samhall in Härnösand, I packed ready-cooked food and beverages in plastic bags that were then distributed by us by car to private persons (mostly elderly) living in Härnösand. We distributed the packages according to a set distribution route each morning. Another operation was elder care. I visited three homes for the elderly run by the City of Härnösand where ten Samhall employees were working on a contract basis, feeding, clothing and washing elderly people. I did not actively participate myself in the work activities as they were regulated by certain rules. Instead, I closely observed how the Samhall employees interacted together and with the individuals they were assisting. A third activity involved cleaning private houses, commissioned by the City of Härnösand. This work involved ordinary cleaning of private persons' homes. I worked in a team of three Samhall employees, both in apartments and in homes.

Stockholm (Southern Sweden)

The first operation was called "book conversion." This entailed "converting" paperbacks into hardcover format to be distributed to libraries, under contract to an organization that sells books from all publishers to libraries in Sweden. The work consisted of ripping the front and back covers off the paperbacks, then sorting the converted books into various staples that were later sent off for reconfiguration into hardback format. I worked in a team consisting of around eight Samhall employees. I then participated as a member of a team working in two stock receiving areas, distributing the items on shelves, sorting them for external distribution and so on. This work was contracted by two corporations that used the stores as their central warehouses in Scandinavia. I worked with around fifteen Samhall employees on different tasks in the two stores. A third activity was cleaning. I carried out cleaning with one or two other employees at companies' premises or in apartment lobbies. Sometimes I cleaned the stairs of tall buildings several days in a row. I also participated in a team that was focused on packaging various items at one of Samhall's units. Together with eight other employees, sitting around a table, I packaged bulbs, condoms, lipstick, pencils and so on that were to be distributed to various customers that had commissioned the packaging work.

Sundsvall (Mid Sweden)

For a number of days I worked at a factory that manufactured ladders. I was given the opportunity to work on the different stages of producing ladders that were sold on the market by Samhall. Each stage consisted of various activities that were carried out by several teams. Later on during this stay, I visited a riding club that employed five Samhall employees on a contract basis. Here, I did not participate in the work activities as I only visited the site for a couple of hours. The employees were working on ordinary tasks related to the maintenance of the horses and buildings. Finally, I visited a site where Samhall employees were sorting clothes on commission from a relief organization. The clothes had been donated by private individuals, and were sorted into bags according to color, size, type (winter, summer) and so on. I observed the work that was carried out in different stations by around forty Samhall employees.

Lund and Malmö (Southern Sweden)

I participated in the production and distribution of food for private persons. The work was carried out in one of Samhall's large-scale kitchens, where I participated in preparing the cooking (for example, by cleaning large amounts of vegetables) and in the cooking itself (for example, broiling meat balls). I worked together with Samhall employees in teams of around three. After having produced the food, it was frozen in parcels according to a specific procedure in which a number of employees were engaged. The parcels were then distributed to clients by car. Then I worked in a team that carried out shopping for everyday commodities in a food store. Together with the other team members, I bought items such as milk, marmalade, butter and yoghurt according to a list drawn up by each client. After having shopped at the food store, we distributed the commodities by car to the clients. Finally, I worked in a cleaning unit. Samhall contracts with clients to take collect dirty laundry, clean it and return it to them. I participated in activities focusing on cleaning and ironing, working in a facility with around forty Samhall employees.

Uppsala (Southern Sweden)

In Uppsala, I participated in the work activities at two Samhall work places. In one of them, the work revolved around sorting and cataloging hospital documents. The work place was located in a major hospital. The Samhall team consisted of around ten persons. At the other site, I worked together with other employees who sorted large amount of documents from various customers that were to be archived electronically, either on CD-ROM or by microfilming. I participated in various activities in different teams that specialized in the relevant activities.

Gävle (Mid Sweden)

In Gävle, Samhall has a large factory that produces metal cabinets and safes. I worked together with Samhall employees carrying out various operations involved in the production of these goods, such as working with a milling-machine, a lathe or painting.

Fagersta (Mid Sweden)

Here, I worked at Samhall's factory producing bathroom cupboards, one of Samhall's best-selling products. The work was similar to that I carried out in Gävle – typical industrial labor activity.

Ludvika (Mid Sweden)

In Ludvika, Samhall produces advanced electrical fittings on contract to a leading design firm in Sweden. As in Gävle and Fagersta, the factory consisted of around 90 employees and the work was organized according to a traditional division of labor. I worked in various teams with various assignments, such as assembly, installation and testing.

Bibliography

Abberley, P. 2002. "Work, Disability, Disabled People and European Social Theory". In C. Barnes, M. Oliver and L. Barton (eds), *Disability Studies Today*. Cambridge: Polity Press, 120–38.

Abrahamson, P. and W. Oorschot. 2003. "The Dutch and Danish Miracles Revisited: A Critical Discussion of Activation Policies in Two Small Welfare States", *Social Policy and Administration*, 37, 288–304.

Albrecht, G., K. Seelman and M. Bury (eds). 2001. *Handbook of Disability Studies*. New York: Paul Chapman.

Ashforth, B.E. and G.E. Kreiner. 1999. "'How Can You Do It?': Dirty Work and the Challenge of Constructing a Positive Identity", *Academy of Management Review*, 24, 413–34.

Aulin, S.-Å. 2001. *Röster från Samhall*. Stockholm: Elanders Gotab.

Bauman, Z. 2007. "Society Enables and Disables", *Scandinavian Journal of Disability Research*, 9, 58–60.

Beatty, C. and S. Fothergill. 2002. "Hidden Unemployment among Men: A Case Study", *Regional Studies*, 36, 811–23.

Beatty, C. and S. Fothergill. 2005. "The Diversion from 'Unemployment' to 'Sickness' across British Regions and Districts", *Regional Studies*, 39: 837–54.

Branson, J. and D. Miller. 2002. *Damned for their Difference: The Cultural Construction of Deaf People as Disabled. A Sociological History*. Washington, DC: Gallaudet.

Brunsson, N. 1989. *The Organization of Hypocrisy*. Chichester: Wiley.

Butcher, T. 2002. *Delivering Welfare*, 2nd edn. Buckingham: Open University Press.

Calmfors, L., A. Forslund and M. Hemström. 2002. *Does Active Labor Market Policy Work? Lessons from the Swedish Experiences*. Uppsala: Institute for Labor Market Policy Evaluation Working Paper 2002:4.

Conrad, P. and J.W. Schneider. 1992. *Deviance and Medicalization*. Philadelphia, PA: Temple University Press.

Considine, M. 2001. *Enterprising States: The Public Management of Welfare-to-Work*. Cambridge: Cambridge University Press.

Corker M. and T. Shakespeare. 2002. *Disability/Postmodernity: Embodying Disability Theory*. London: Continuum.

Crawford, R. 2006. "Health as Meaningful Practice", *Health*, 10, 401–20.

De Lathouwer, L. 2005. "Reforming the Passive Welfare State: Belgium's New Income Arrangements to Make Work Pay in International Perspective". In P. Saunders (ed.), *Welfare to Work in Practice: Social Security and Participation in Economic and Social Life*. Aldershot: Ashgate, 129–54.

De Mooij, R.A. 1999. "Disability Benefits and Hidden Unemployment in The Netherlands", *Journal of Policy Modeling*, 21, 695–713.

Dean, M. 1995. "Governing the Unemployed Self in an Active Society", *Economy and Society*, 24, 559–83.

Dick, P. 2005. "Dirty Work Designations: How Police Officers Account for their use of Coercive Force", *Human Relations*, 58, 1, 363–90.

Douglas, M. 2002. *Purity and Danger*. London: Routledge.

Drake, R.F. 1999. *Understanding Disability Policies*. London: Macmillan.

Elm Larsen, J. 2005. "The Active Society and Activation Policy: Ideologies, Contexts and Effects". In J. Goul Andersen, A.-M. Guillemard, P.H. Jensen and B. Pfau-Effinger (eds), *The Changing Face of Welfare: Consequences and Outcomes from a Citizen Perspective*. Bristol: The Policy Press, 135–50.

Emerson, R.M. and M. Pollner. 1975. "Dirty Work Designations: Their Features and Consequences in a Psychiatric Setting", *Social Problems*, 23, 243–54.

Fieldhouse, E. and E. Hollywood. 1999. "Life after Mining: Hidden Unemployment and Changing Patterns of Economic Activity Amongst Miners in England and Wales, 1981–1991", *Work, Employment and Society*, 13, 483–502.

Fredriksson, P. and P. Johansson. 2003. *Employment, Mobility and Active Labor Market Programs*. Uppsala: Institute for Labor Market Policy Evaluation Working Paper 2003:3.

Fujiura, G.T. and V. Rutkowski-Kmitta. 2001. "Counting Disability". In Albrecht, G., K. Seelman and M. Bury (eds) (2001), *Handbook of Disability Studies*. New York: Paul Chapman, 69–96.

Garraty, J.A. 1978. *Unemployment in History*. New York: Harper & Row.

Garsten, C. and K. Jacobsson. 2004. "Learning to be Employable: An Introduction". In C. Garsten and K. Jacobsson (eds), *Learning to be Employable: New Agendas on Work, Responsibility and Learning in a Globalizing World*. Houndmills: Palgrave, 1–22.

Gilbert, N. 2005. "Protection to Activation: The Apotheosis of Work". In P. Saunders (ed.), *Welfare to Work in Practice: Social Security and Participation in Economic and Social Life*. Aldershot: Ashgate, 9–22.

Glennerster, H. 1999. "Which Welfare States are Most Likely to Survive?", *International Review of Social Welfare*, 8, 2–13.

Goffman, E. 1961. *Asylums: Essays on the Social Situation of Mental Patients and Other Inmates*. New York: Anchor.

Goul Andersen, J., A.-M. Guillemard, P.H. Jensen and B. Pfau-Effinger (eds) 2005. *The Changing Face of Welfare: Consequences and Outcomes from a Citizen Perspective*. Bristol: The Policy Press.

Gummer, B. 1990. *The Politics of Social Administration: Managing Organizational Politics in Social Agencies*. Englewood Cliffs, NJ: Prentice-Hall.

Hammersley, M. and P. Atkinson. 1995. *Ethnography: Principles in Practice*, 2nd edn. London: Routledge.

Hansen, H., P. Hespanha, C. Machado and R. Van Berkel. 2002. "Inclusion through Participation? Active Social Policies in the EU and Empirical Observations from Case Studies into Types of Work". In R. Van Berkel and I. Hornemann Moller (eds), *Active Social Policies in the EU: Inclusion through Participation?* Bristol: The Policy Press, 103–36.

Holmqvist, M. 2005. *Samhall: Att bli normal i en onormal organisation.* Stockholm: SNS Förlag.

Holmqvist, M. 2008. *The Institutionalization of Social Welfare: A Study of Medicalizing Management.* New York: Routledge.

Hughes, E.C. 1951. "Work and the Self". In J.H. Rohrer and M. Sherif (eds), *Social Psychology at the Crossroads.* New York: Harper, 312–23.

Hughes, E.C. 1962. "Good People and Dirty Work", *Social Problems*, 10, 3–11.

Hughes, E.C. 1971. *The Sociological Eye: Selected Papers.* Chicago, IL: Aldine.

Hvinden, B., M. Heikkilä and I. Kankare. 2001. "Towards Activation? The Changing Relationship between Social Protection and Employment in Western Europe". In M. Kautto, J. Fritzell, B. Hvinden, J. Kvist and H. Uusitalo (eds), *Nordic Welfare States in the European Context.* London: Routledge, 168–97.

Janoski, T. 1990. *The Political Economy of Unemployment: Active Labor Market Policy in West Germany and the United States.* Berkeley, CA: University of California Press.

Jensen, P.H. and B. Pfau-Effinger. 2005. "'Active' Citizenship: The New Face of Welfare". In J. Goul Andersen, A.-M. Guillemard, P.H. Jensen and B. Pfau-Effinger (eds), *The Changing Face of Welfare. Consequences and Outcomes from a Citizen Perspective.* Bristol: The Policy Press, 1–14.

Johansson, P. and P. Skedinger. 2005. *Are Objective, Official Measures of Disability Reliable?* Uppsala: Institute for Labor Market Policy Evaluation Working Paper 2005:14.

Kvist, J. 2002. "Activating Welfare States: How Social Policies can Promote Employment". In J. Clasen (ed.), *What Future for Social Security?* The Hague: Kluwer Law International.

Lane, H. 1997. "Construction of Deafness". In L.J. Davis (ed.), *The Disability Studies Reader.* London: Routledge, 153–71.

Lange, T. and Y. Georgellis (eds). 2007. *Active Labor Market Policies and Unemployment.* Bradford: Emerald.

Lincoln, Y.S. and E.G. Guba. 1985. *Naturalistic Inquiry.* London: Sage.

Lindert, P.H. 2004. *Growing Public.* Cambridge: Cambridge University Press.

Lister, R. 1998. "From Equality to Social Inclusion: New Labor and the Welfare State", *Critical Social Policy*, 55, 215–25.

Lødemel, I. and H. Trickey. 2001. *"An Offer You Can't Refuse": Workfare in International Perspective.* Bristol: The Policy Press.

OECD. 2003. *Transforming Disability into Ability: Policies to Promote Work and Income Security for Disabled People.* Paris: Organization for Economic Cooperation and Development.

Oorschot, W. and B. Hvinden. 2001. *Disability Policies in European Countries.* The Hague: Kluwer Law International.

Overbye, E. 2005. "Dilemmas in Disability Activation and How Scandinavians Try to Live with Them". In P. Saunders (ed.), *Welfare to Work in Practice: Social Security and Participation in Economic and Social Life*. Aldershot: Ashgate, 155–72.

Rådahl, E. 1990. *Löftesfabriken: Samhall i närbild*. Stockholm: Pandemos.

Resnick, H. and R.J. Patti (eds). 1980. *Change from Within: Humanizing Social Welfare Organizations*. Philadelphia, PA: Temple University Press.

Saunders, P. 2005. "Welfare to Work in Practice: Introduction and Overview". In P. Saunders (ed.), *Welfare to Work in Practice: Social Security and Participation in Economic and Social Life*. Aldershot: Ashgate, 1–8.

Schram, S.F. 2000. "In the Clinic. The Medicalization of Welfare", *Social Text*, 18, 81–107.

Serrano Pascual, A. 2007. "Reshaping Welfare States: Activation Regimes in Europe". In A. Serrano Pascual and L. Magnusson (eds), *Reshaping Welfare States and Activation Regimes in Europe*. Brussels: Peter Lang, 11–34.

Shildrick, M. and J. Price. 1996. "Breaking the Boundaries of the Broken Body", *Disability and Society*, 2, 93–113.

Silverman, D. 2006. *Interpreting Qualitative Data: Methods for Analyzing Talk, Text and Interaction*, 3rd edn. London: Sage.

Spradley, J.P. 1979. *The Ethnographic Interview*. Belmont, CA: Wadsworth.

Strauss, A. and J. Corbin. 1998. *Basics of Qualitative Research: Techniques and Procedures for Developing Grounded Theory*, 2nd edn. London: Sage.

Thomas, C. 2004. "How is Disability Understood? An Examination of Sociological Approaches", *Disability and Society*, 19, 569–583.

Van Berkel, R. and I. Hornemann Moller. 2002. "The Concept of Activation". In R. Van Berkel and I. Hornemann Moller (eds), *Active Social Policies in the EU: Inclusion through Participation?* Bristol: The Policy Press, 45–72.

Van Berkel, R., I. Hornemann Moller and C.C. Williams. 2002. "The Concept of Inclusion/exclusion and the Concept of Work". In R. Van Berkel and I. Hornemann Moller (eds), *Active Social Policies in the EU: Inclusion through Participation?* Bristol: The Policy Press, 15–44.

Wadensjö, E. 2007. "Activation Policy in Sweden". In A. Serrano Pascual and L. Magnusson (eds), *Reshaping Welfare States and Activation Regimes in Europe*. Brussels: Peter Lang, 127–44.

Walters, W. 1997. "The 'Active Society': New Designs for Social Policy", *Policy and Politics*, 25, 221–34.

Williams, S. 1999. "Is Anybody There? Critical Realism, Chronic Illness and the Disability Debate", *Sociology of Health and Illness*, 21, 797–819.

Index